BUST THOSE MANAGEMENT MYTHS

What We Get Wrong About Planning, Leading, Measuring, and More

HENRY MINTZBERG

Berrett-Koehler
PUBLISHERS

Berrett-Koehler Publishers, Inc.
1333 Broadway, Suite P100
Oakland, CA 94612-1921
(510) 817-2277
bkconnection.com

Ordering Information
Quantity sales. Special discounts are available on quantity purchases by corporations, associations, individuals, and others. For details, please go to bkconnection.com to see our bulk discounts or contact bookorders@bkpub.com for more information.
Textbook exam/desk copies. Please consult the General FAQ at bkconnection.com.
Bookstore orders for trade or textbook use. For print books, please contact Penguin Random House Publisher Services at customerservice@penguinrandomhouse.com. For ebooks, contact your favorite distributor.

Distributed to the US trade and internationally by Penguin Random House Publisher Services.

The authorized representative in the EU for product safety and compliance is EU Compliance Partner, Pärnu mnt. 139b-14, 11317 Tallinn, Estonia, www.eucompliancepartner.com, +372 5368 65 02.

Printed in the United States of America

Berrett-Koehler books are printed on long-lasting acid-free paper. When it is available, we choose paper that has been manufactured by environmentally responsible processes. These may include using trees grown in sustainable forests, incorporating recycled paper, minimizing chlorine in bleaching, or recycling the energy produced at the paper mill.

Library of Congress Cataloging-in-Publication Data
Names: Mintzberg, Henry author
Title: Bust those management myths : what we get wrong about planning, leading, measuring, and more / Henry Mintzberg.
Description: First edition. | Oakland, CA : Berrett-Koehler Publishers, Inc., [2026] | Includes bibliographical references and index.
Identifiers: LCCN 2026012679 (print) | LCCN 2026012680 (ebook) | ISBN 9798890571724 paperback | ISBN 9798890571731 pdf | ISBN 9798890571748 epub
Subjects: LCSH: Leadership | Management | Organizational behavior
Classification: LCC HD57.7 .M5595 2026 (print) | LCC HD57.7 (ebook)
LC record available at https://lccn.loc.gov/2026012679
LC ebook record available at https://lccn.loc.gov/2026012680

First Edition

35 34 33 32 31 30 29 28 27 26 10 9 8 7 6 5 4 3 2 1

Book production: BookMatters
Cover design: Ashley Ingram

I dedicate this book to the communityship that is Berrett-Koehler, especially Jeevan, the self-described "cranky editorial guy," who serendipitously suggested I do this book, and then provided canny counsel to advance it; Neal, who joined him in championing this book, and then organized it empathetically; and Steve, who established this communityship by dodging these myths, while deMYTHtifying publishing itself.[1]

Thank you, Susie, Santa, and Dulcie, for your copious, caring contributions.

Contents

deMYTHtify! (an Introduction) 1

I The Myth of Leadership 5

MYTH 1: Lofty leadership tops mere management. 5

II Two Myths of Organizing 13

MYTH 2: Organizations have tops, middles, and (therefore) bottoms. 13

MYTH 3: There is one best way to organize. 23

III Three Myths of Managing 39

MYTH 4: Management is a profession that relies on the evidence of analysis. 39

MYTH 5: MBA education prepares students to manage. 48

MYTH 6: Managers plan, organize, coordinate, and control (i.e., they control, control, control, and control). 61

IV Three Myths About Analyzing 81

MYTH 7: If you can't measure it, you can't manage it. 81

MYTH 8: Proper strategies are planned. 94

MYTH 9: To make decisions, think in order to act. 113

V The Mother of All Myths 127

MYTH 10: Our theory is true. 127

Additional Insights Available on MythSite.org 135

Notes 137

Index 145

About the Author 151

deMYTHtify! *(an Introduction)*

deMYTHtify—that's what I do. Feel free to call me Henry MythBurst.

I have spent a lifetime trying to bust and burst every management myth in sight, to take them out of sight, for the sake of insight. In the process, I have set out to reframe managing and measuring, strategy and structure, lofty leadership and lowly politics. If we can refresh our laptops, surely, we can refresh our heads.

Hence, I offer this book as a collection of corrections—my freshest ideas, so to speak—mostly excerpted from my books and blogs, articles and utterances. Together, we will turn over the rocks that cover ten myths, to understand what is happening underneath. Each *Myth* is discussed together with a corresponding *deMyth*, elaborated from my research and writing over the years. At the end of the discussion of each of the Myths and deMyths, I have included a few *Insights*—compelling stories from my work that illustrate the text. (Other Insights that may be of interest to some readers can be found on MythSite .org, a sort of second book for whoever wants more. These are listed at the end of the book.)

We begin with the widespread myth of lofty leadership, that it is somehow better than mere management. This has been awfully destructive of leadership as well as management. Managing and leading are two sides of the same job: managers have to lead; leaders have to manage.

Next come two myths of organizing—that organizations have tops, middles, and (therefore) bottoms, and that there is one best way to organize. That way usually amounts to bureaucracy (by some other name) which, I assure you, is not the best way to organize, although it is one of the fundamental ways to do so. To think past hierarchical leadership, how about engaged *communityship*?

Three myths of managing follow. First is that management is a profession that relies on the evidence of analysis, whereas I maintain that management is a practice grounded in experience. Second is that the conventional MBA prepares students to manage everything, while we have more than enough evidence to conclude that this kind of education distorts the practice of managing, whereas social learning that uses managers' experience enhances it. The third myth of managing is that managers plan, organize, coordinate, and control (i.e., control, control, control, and control). In truth, managers have trouble controlling their own jobs, which entails a lot more than controlling.

From here, we consider three myths of analyzing. The refrain that "if you can't measure it, you can't manage it" is just plain silly. Whoever measured management, let alone measurement? Then there is the widespread myth that proper strategies are planned. Sorry, but interesting strategies are learned. And third, to make decisions, we are supposed to think before we act. There are times, however, when we do better by acting in order to think, even by seeing in order to act.

Last but most comes the mother of all myths—in management and elsewhere—that our own theory is true. No theory is true—all are myths in one way or another—although some can sometimes be useful.

The Myth of Leadership

Myth 1 Lofty leadership tops mere management.

deMyth 1 Leadership and management are two sides of the same job—managers have to lead; leaders have to manage.

Ever since Warren Bennis claimed a half century ago that leaders "do the right things" while managers "do things right," we have been mired in the myth that leadership is somehow superior to management.[2] Leaders take the long view, see the big picture, from on top; managers administer the consequences down below. So simple. Until we lift the rock over lofty leadership, to uncover the ground of regular managing.

> John Cleghorn, CEO of the Royal Bank of Canada, called the office one day on his way to the airport to report a broken ATM machine. The bank had thousands of such machines. Why was the chief bothering to report one? Was he micromanaging? Maybe he was leading by managing, namely, setting an example for others to follow: keep your eyes open even for small problems.

> Gord Irwin was the Front Country Manager of the Banff National Park—an operations manager, in charge of the "civilized" part of the park, the roads, etc. He was concerned about the long-term consequences of a parking lot expansion at a ski hill. Was Gord pretending to lead? Or was he doing something right in the short term, for the sake of the long term?

Hence, I propose an end to the myth that leadership is separate from management, and somehow superior. This is depreciating management all right, but leadership more so. We may obsess about being overmanaged, but now we are *over-led.*

Would you like to be managed by someone who doesn't lead? That could be awfully discouraging. Well then, why would you want to be led by someone who doesn't manage? They wouldn't know what's going on. Management is about rolling up your sleeves to find out what's going on. As Jim March of Stanford University put it, "leadership involves plumbing as well as poetry."[3]

Here are a few problems with the concept of leadership in general.

Leadership is individual, but organizations are communal. Say the word *leader,* or *leadership,* and what comes to mind is a single individual—the proverbial maestro on the podium, alone, above the fray. But the fray is the organization, a form of community. No wonder we get so much narcissism in positions of power—from dominating dictators to dictating directors. Is the president the state? Is the CEO the company?

Individualism has two very different meanings: acting for

oneself and thinking for oneself. Ironically, the more we get of leadership acting for itself, the less we get of it thinking for itself—for example, by accepting outsized pay packages that undermine the spirit of the enterprise. This comes in the name of leadership, but it's followership.

Micro-managing may be bad, but macro-leading can be worse. And worst of all are macro-*leaders* who *micro-manage*. We make a great fuss these days about micro-managing—managers who meddle when they should stay clear, to allow other people to get on with their work. Such managers can get so enmeshed in the details that they lose sight of the big picture. But worse still can be macro-leading—people too removed to be able to create any picture at all. This leaves everyone wandering around, wondering where to go.

While micro-managing may undermine the efforts of certain managers, macro-leading can undermine the spirit of the entire organization. Beware especially of the macro-leaders who micro-manage, as they flit back and forth between abstract generalities that help no one and specific interruptions that hinder everyone, with a kind of no-vision land in between.

The "big picture" of an organization has to be painted with the little brushstrokes of everyday experience. It may seem to appear all at once, as if immaculately conceived, but, more commonly, it builds over time, in the head of a "visionary" who is deeply engaged with the specifics of the organization.

In contrast, disengaged people who macro-lead are inclined to seize on some abstraction, say, that the organization has to be "the biggest." A number is not a vision. And when that number is decomposed into targets for everyone else to meet, the whole place gets reduced to management by remote control—hands off everything except the numbers.

Hence, we shall have to recognize that leadership apart from management has become the problem more than the solution. Thus, the more we obsess about leadership, the less of it we get. True leadership is a fine idea when practiced with management. **We don't need lofty leadership, seen as superior to mere management. We need managers who *lead*, by engaging themselves to engage others, to help release the energy that exists naturally within people.** (See Table M1.1)

TABLE M1.1. Lofty leadership or engaging management?

LOFTY LEADERSHIP	ENGAGING MANAGEMENT
1. Leaders are important people, quite apart from others who develop products and deliver services.	1. Managers are important to the extent that they help other people to be important.
2. The higher "up" these leaders go, the more important they become. At the "top," the CEO *is* the organization.	2. An organization is an interacting network, not a vertical hierarchy. Effective managers work throughout; they don't sit "on top."
3. Down the hierarchy comes the strategy—clear, deliberate, and bold—emanating from the chief who takes the dramatic acts. Everyone else *implements*.	3. Out of the network emerge strategies, as engaged people solve little problems that can grow into big pictures.
4. To lead is to make decisions and allocate resources—including those human resources. Leadership thus means calculating, based on facts, from analysis.	4. To manage is to help bring out the energy that exists naturally within people. Managing thus means engaging, based on judgment, rooted in experience.
5. Leadership is thrust upon those who thrust their will on others.	5. Leadership is a sacred trust earned from the respect of others.

Two Insights to deMYTHtify Lofty Leadership

The first Insight is an apocryphal letter to the board from a CEO who deserves the label leader. *But don't look for it in the boardroom minutes. The second explains why managing has to be about eating scrambled eggs.*

A Leader Letter to the Board[4]

Dear Members of the Board,

I am writing to you with a proposal that may seem radical, but is, in fact, conservative. That is because my primary concern as CEO is to conserve this company as a healthy enterprise. You are now paying me so much that I can no longer manage this company properly. I hereby request that you cut my salary substantially and eliminate my bonuses.

We have talked a great deal about teamwork in our enterprise, that our people are all in this together. So why am I singled out by virtue of my compensation? Bonuses are the worst part of it. Like everyone else here, I am paid to do my job. Why should I be paid extra to do it well? If I believe in this company, I buy the stock. If I don't, I quit. The misguided assumption behind these bonuses is that I, as CEO, do it all.

Now I am getting hate mail from our employees about my pay. This is certainly disconcerting, but more so is that I have no reasonable reply, short of claiming that I must be several hundred times more important than they are. Is this leadership?

We have had a good deal of discussion at our board meetings about the long-term health of this company. Why, then, am I being rewarded for short-term gains in the stock price? You all know perfectly well that I can use all kinds of tricks to drive up that price, while destroying real value—and doing a number on our economy in the process.

Ever since we started this Shareholder *Value* nonsense, our values have gone to hell. The frontline employees tell me that this gets in the way of serving customers: they are expected to see $$$ out there, not people. As one put it to me recently: "With all this counting, we don't count. So why should we care?"

I have always prided myself in being a risk taker; that is one reason you put me in this job. So how come I cash in big when the stock price goes up but pay back nothing when it goes down? Some risk taker! You know what? I'm tired of being a hypocrite.

I know the excuse we have been using all along: that I am just being compensated to keep up with other CEOs. This makes me a follower, not a leader. Enough of this complicity in behavior that we all know to be shameful. My compensation is not a trophy but a message about the culture we are trying to build in this company.

So, please, help me to concentrate on managing this company as it should be managed.

Sincerely,
Your CEO

Managing Scrambled Eggs[5]

Here is a quintessential story of lofty leadership. The CEO led and the airline crashed—all because of the scrambled eggs, which he should have been micro-eating.

One morning, years ago, I flew Eastern Airlines from Montreal to New York. It was the largest airline in the world at the time, but it was soon to go belly up.

They served food in those days, well sort of—something they called "scrambled eggs." I said to the flight attendant: "I've eaten some awfully bad things in airplanes, but this has to be the worst."

"I know," she replied, "we keep telling them; they won't listen."

Now how could this be? If they were running a cemetery, I could understand the difficulties of communicating with the customers. But an airline? Whenever I encounter awful service or a badly designed product, I wonder if the management is living the experience or reading the financial statements?

The financial analysts were certainly reading those statements, and probably explaining the airline's problems in terms of load factors and the like. Don't believe a number of it. Eastern Airlines went belly up because of its scrambled eggs.

Some years later, after telling this story to a group of managers, one of them, from IBM, came up to tell me this story. The CEO of Eastern Airlines came rushing in at the last minute for a flight. First class was full, so they bumped a paying customer to put him where I guess he had become accustomed. Apparently feeling guilty, he reportedly made his way to Economy Class to apologize, introducing himself as the CEO of the airline, only to be introduced to the president of IBM.

Now, don't get this wrong. The problem was not about who was bumped. Quite the contrary, status was the problem: first-class leading mattered more than simply managing. Managing is not about sitting where you have become accustomed. It's about eating the scrambled eggs.

Two Myths of Organizing

Myth 2 **Organizations have tops, middles, and (therefore) bottoms.**

deMyth 2 **Beyond hierarchical leadership, organizations need engaged communityship.**

How come we say "top management" and "middle management" but never "bottom management"? Could this be telling us something: that we need to rid ourselves of a vocabulary that distorts behavior in organizations?

My point is simple: **Top-middle-bottom is a misguided metaphor, revealing our obsession with hierarchy.** How can anyone keep on top of what's going on in an organization when they see themselves on top of it, namely out of the action?

On top of *what*? The headquarters building, for one thing—is this for a better view? The view is actually worse: managers who see themselves on top of their organization see everything in general but nothing in particular. In other words, top is the worst place from which to manage an organization, let alone lead it.

But most evidently, *top* means on top of the organization chart. (See Figure M2.1.) Visit an organization, ask to see a picture of

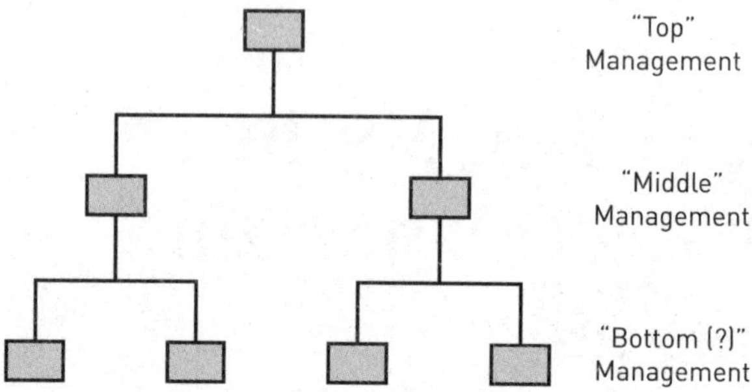

FIGURE M2.1. **An Organization?**

the place, and this may well be the only one they have available. This stacking of boxes—"superiors" over "subordinates"—tells us who sits on top of whom, but not who talks with whom, and about what.

The next time you see one of these charts like Figure M2.1, cover the name on the organization and try to figure out what it actually does for a living: the products it makes, the services it renders. Using the chart to find your way around an organization is like using a list of counselors to find your way around a city.

And then we have those ubiquitous *reorganizations*. They are so popular because they are so easy. Change a few names and titles on a piece of paper and off you go—sending everybody into utter confusion. (The National Health Service of England has reorganized so often that an editorial in the *British Medical Journal* once described it as being in a state of constant "redisorganization."[6]) So let's reorganize our heads by seeing organizations differently, starting with slabs beyond silos, and then hubs, webs, and sets beyond chains.

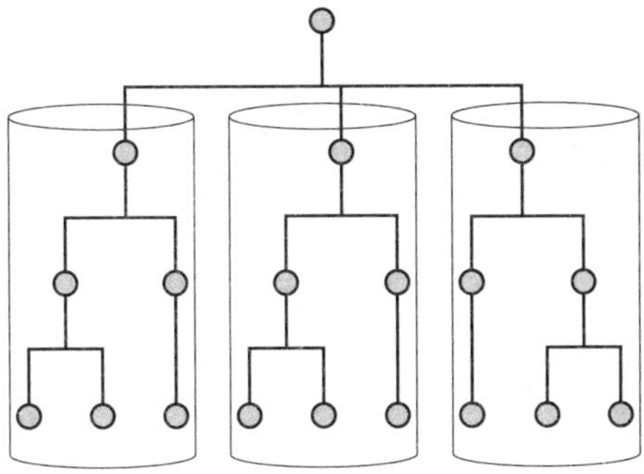

FIGURE M2.2. Silos in Organizations

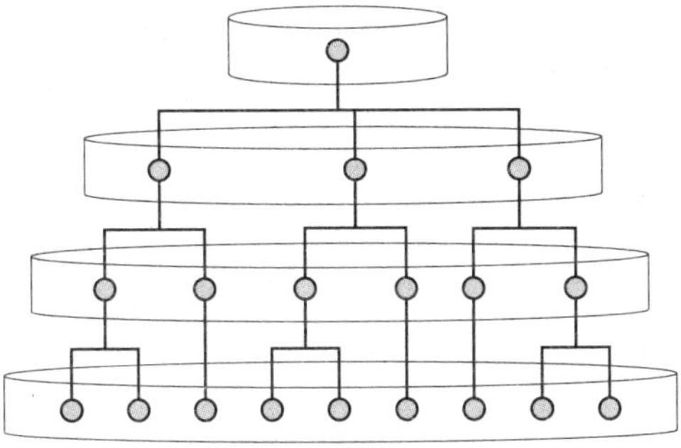

FIGURE M2.3. Slabs in Organizations

Slabs Across the Silos

We all know about the *silos* in organizations: those vertical impediments to horizontal communication across units. (See Figure M2.2.) We must also understand the *slabs*: those horizontal impediments to communicating vertically between levels in the hierarchy. (See Figure M2.3.) The "glass ceilings" that keep women from advancing up the hierarchy is an example. So are the concrete floors that sometimes separate different levels of management.

We may need silos for the sake of specialization in our organizations, so long as they are permeable, to allow for collaboration. But do we really need all those slabs? For example, must the CEO, COO, CFO, etc., all sit on their own floor, apart from everyone else? Years ago, when the Sears retail chain moved out of its tower in Chicago, the tallest building in the world at the time, the CEO explained that "We had become a vertical culture." It's interesting how people who will happily walk some distance horizontally hesitate to climb even a single flight of stairs.

Imagine if the CO-somethings all came down from atop their tower to sit next to people with a different perspective? Kao, a Japanese cosmetics company, became famous for running its meetings in open spaces so that anyone going by could join: a foreman at the executive committee, an executive at a factory meeting. Let's bust the slabs to acknowledge that they are mere figments of our lack of imagination.

Chains, Hubs, Webs, and Sets

Another way to get past all this top to bottom stuff is to *see* the different ways that activities in organizations connect—as chains, hubs, webs, and sets.

Consider a wedding, which is an organization of sorts. The event itself is a hub, a central place to which people come from their homes to celebrate. At the buffet table, they form a chain, advancing in single file from one dish to the next. When they sit back at their various tables, these form a set in the room. And during the meal, at each table, and later, during the dancing, the guests become a web—an interacting network of communication, every which way. To use more conventional examples,

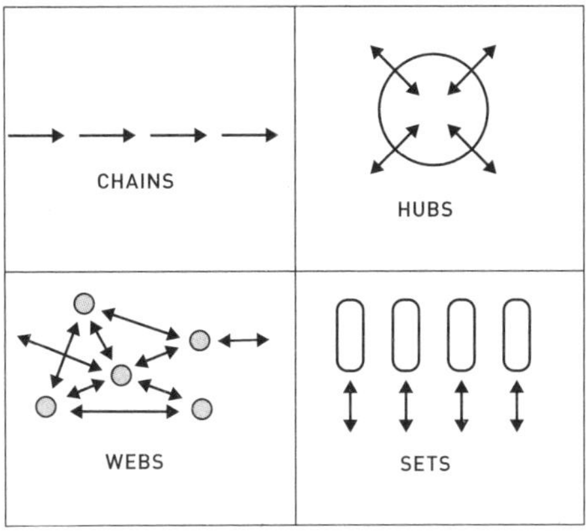

an automobile assembly line is a chain, an airport is a hub, a film crew works like a web, and professors working apart in the university form a set.

For some reason, perhaps because of our propensity to be linear, we tend to favor chains. For example, the organization chart is a vertical chain, formally known as the *chain of command*. These days, it is often considered to sit over some sort of horizontal chain of operations—the "value chain," the "supply chain," the "operating chain," and so on. This may be fine for assembling automobiles, but must every flow be linear? A "chain" of retail stores is hardly a chain; it's more a set of separate stores. Even medical specialists in a hospital—say, pediatricians and geriatricians—can be described as a set: how much do they share besides a parking lot? Each patient in a bed, however, is a hub, to whom come most of their services—nursing, medicine, food, oxygen. This is not so for some research projects in the hospital, whose members interact in a web of open communication.

These four different organizational models—chains, hubs, webs, and sets—enable us to see the place of managers in

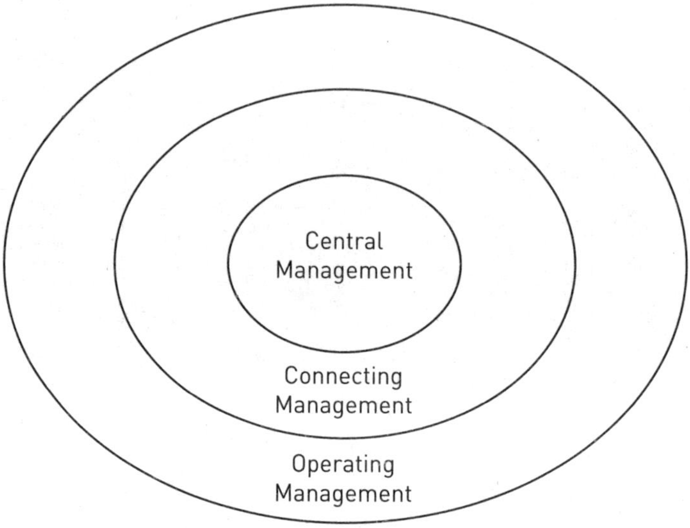

FIGURE M2.4. **Managing Around**

organizations differently. In the chain of command, they sit on top—a manager over each unit and a manager over each manager. In a hub, they sit at the center, if you like, of a circle, to replace the chart, as shown in Figure M2.4. In her book *The Female Advantage: Women's Ways of Leadership*, Sally Helgesen found that women managers "referred to themselves as being in the middle of things. Not on top but in the center; not reaching down, but reaching out."[7] If we put the manager in the center of a web, however, we *centralize* it, as a hub, which can restrict communication. Instead, to know what's going on in a web, the manager has to be seen as operating throughout. And in a set? Significantly, they face out, as do hospital managers when they connect with funders.

So **maybe it's time to bust the chain and burst the chart by opening them up to the richer vocabulary of hubs, webs, and sets, alongside chains**, as we shall do in the next myth. (See the Insight "Organigraphs" as an alternative depiction of organizations—as the flow of activities—on MythSite.org.)

But one thing is still missing. The chart may depict the organization as a bunch of bones, but where is the heart and soul of the place, the life force that holds everything together? This is where communityship comes in.

Communityship Beyond Leadership

Effective organizations have souls, much as interesting people have personalities. Hence, instead of *leadership above all*, we need to recognize *communityship of all*.[8]

There is no such word in the English language, so I created it, to help put leadership in its place, which, in part, is to enhance the organization as a community of engaged human beings, rather than as a hierarchy of passive human resources.

Vibrant organizations have souls; communityship is that soul—the collective spirit that engages their people naturally, instead of having to be formally empowered. They respect the organization because the organization respects them, for their expertise and experience, as members of a community, where continuous care matters more than intermittent cure. (By the way, if you think a network is a community, try asking your Facebook friends to help paint your house. Networks connect; communities care, ss discussed in the Insight entitled Networks are not Communities on MythSite.org.)

How can we recognize communityship? That's easy. It strikes us the moment we walk into a place: the energy of the people, their delight in working there—just like a sports team that comes out of nowhere to win a championship. There is a famous line in a Molière play about a character who discovers that he has been speaking "prose" all his life. Well, it's time for us to discover that **many of our great organizations have been living communityship all their lives.**

Communityship flattens the conventional hierarchy, turning a vertical chain of ordered communication into a flexible web of collaboration. Anyone with appropriate experience in an appropriate place can participate in certain decisions that are normally reserved for managers. This is called *distributed management*. (Another Insight on MythSite.org, "Selecting Flawed Managers," discusses distributing the decision to select managers.) After all, if bees can do distributed management, why not we human beings?

> Scout bees now fly out from the bivouac in all directions in the search for a new permanent nest site. When a suitable site is found [...] the scouts return and signal the direction and distance of the find [...] Different scouts may announce different sites simultaneously, and a contest ensues. Finally the site being advertised most vigorously by the largest number of workers wins, and the entire swarm flies off to it [the queen bee in tow].[9]

Two Insights to deMYTHtify Top to Bottom

The first Insight contrasts two hotels, with and without soul. The second shows how easy it is to kill communityship.

Hotels With and Without Soul[10]

My daughter Lisa once left me a note in a shoe that read "Souls need fixing." Little did she know (or, at the time, how to spell).

Years later, the two of us went to the north of England, me to meet colleagues in our international program for managers (a program designed *with soul*, described in Myth 5). We stayed at one of those corporate hotels—everything proper, but no spirit, no soul: mediocre food, high staff turnover, the rest ordinary.

After the meeting, we went to the English Lake District to check out another hotel to be used later in the program. We walked in and fell in love with the place instantly. Beautifully appointed, perfectly cared for, a genuinely enthusiastic staff—this hotel was loaded with soul. No "greeter" here dispensing programmed care.

"What's it mean to have soul?" Lisa asked. "You know it when you see it," I replied. I asked a waiter about hiking trails. He didn't know, so he fetched the manager of the hotel, who came minutes later, in no rush to cut the conversation short.

Later, I chatted with a young woman at reception. "The throw pillows on the bed are really beautiful," I said. "Yes," she replied, "the owner cares for every detail—she picked those pillows herself." "How long have you been here?" I asked. "Four years," she said proudly, and then rattled off the tenures of the senior staff: the manager, fourteen years; the assistant manager, twelve years; the head of sales, a little less.

Why can't all organizations be like this? Most people—employees, customers, managers—want to care, given half a chance. We human beings have souls, so why not our organizations? Why do we build so many great institutions only to let them wither under the control of people who should never have been allowed to manage anything? Souls really *do* need fixing, in organizations no less than shoes.

Killing Communityship[11]

Building communityship may take time, but killing it is quickly done.

When we asked the participants in our McGill health care management program to share stories about their experiences, an obstetrician told about the time when he was shuttling as a resident between the wards of two different hospitals. He and his colleagues "loved working" in one of them. It was a "happy" place, thanks to a head nurse who cared. She was understanding, respectful of everyone, intent on promoting collaboration between doctors and nurses. The place had soul.

Then she retired and was replaced by someone qualified in nursing, with a master's degree in management. Without "any conversation . . . she started questioning everything." She was strict with the nurses, for example, arriving early to check who came late. Where there used to be chatting and laughing at the start of shifts, he said, "It became normal for us to see one nurse crying" because of some comment by the new manager.

Morale plummeted, and soon that spread to the physicians: "It took two to three months to destroy that amazing family. . . . We used to compete to go to that hospital; [later] we didn't want to go there anymore." Yet "the higher authority didn't intervene, or maybe was not aware" of what was going on. Were they any better?

Myth 3 There is one best way to organize.

deMyth 3 There are a few fundamental ways to organize.

One best way to organize?[12] Sure, just like one best way to make matzo balls. The myths of this book, such as leadership on top, are all one-best ways, each in their own way.

In 1911, Frederick Taylor published a book entitled *The Principles of Scientific Management* where he proposed the "one best method."[13] His method was to stand over workers with a stopwatch, micro-analyze every detail of their work—treating them as hands without heads—and reconfigure the work for greater efficiency. We don't do this much anymore, but we certainly keep subscribing to some "one best way" or other, as we now call it, for most everything in organizations, from strategy to structure, for food banks and factory farms. Strategic planning, everyone?

Should your local hospital be managed as a focused factory, as one of Harvard's gurus on managing health care claimed?[14] Likewise, should government—and everything else—be managed like a business? (See "Business as the Best Way?" on MythSite.org.) Maybe the best ways of managing so much business today are not the best even for business.

Magazine articles for managers have long presented most every new technique as the latest, hottest, one best way—for example, empowering everyone one year, and downsizing them all the next. I believe that all these articles should have a skull and crossbones printed at the top, with something like this: WARNING: For bureaucracies only. Not to be taken by adhocracies.

Whatever is "hot" is probably wrong, at least for those organizations that adopt it mindlessly. Even if it may be good, mindless application will render it bad. Likewise, with any "best practice" that does not specify where or when. Fashion may have its boutiques of haute couture, but do organizations need boutiques of haute structure—those consulting firms that foist the latest structural fashion on all their clients? As we shall discuss in the following myths, **basic managing is *fundamental*, not *fashionable*.**

There is "one best way" to organize that has long been the most fashionable. It amounts to bureaucracy, but usually with some other label, like *efficiency*. This way has actually been with us for quite some time, as in this description of a temple in ancient Mesopotamia: "All operations were carried out according to predetermined plan. . . . Directions were numerous and explicit, and the work to be done was structured according to task and specialty. The performance of subordinance was closely and efficiently supervised."[15]

These remain the imperatives of bureaucracy—in effect, specialize, standardize, centralize, analyze, and especially, measure and program everything in sight. There is nothing wrong with this, if the purpose of an organization is to mass produce as efficiently as possible. How else to sell fast food, other than through programming every detail—including ourselves as customers, who duly clear our tables after eating. Of course, if you did this in a gourmet restaurant, you might get some strange looks. That's because these restaurants are about proficiency more than efficiency; they are meritocracies

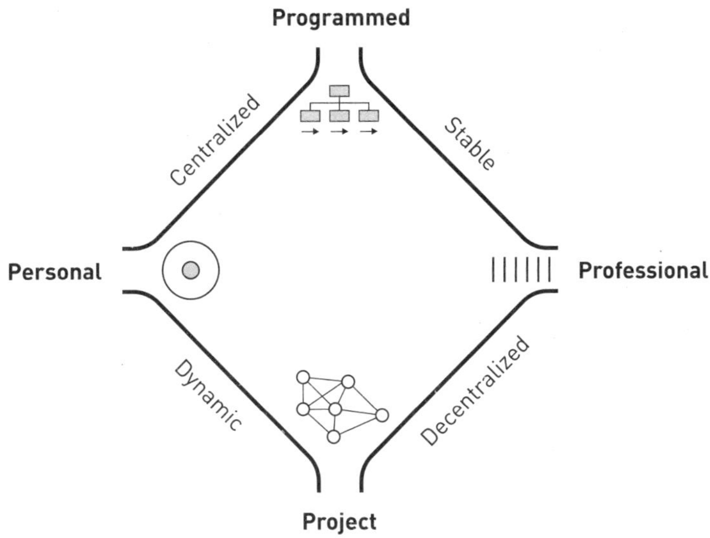

FIGURE M3.1. Four Fundamental Forms of Organizing

more than bureaucracies. Other restaurants can be different again. On the beach, you might find a lobster shack owned by an individual who manages it all personally, as a kind of autocracy. And then there is a catered banquet, say at a wedding: it is customized to this one particular event—as an adhocracy.

Hence, we can no more find one best way to structure all these restaurants than we can find one best chef to cook in all of them. My point is that, while there may be no one best way to organize, there can be several fundamental ways to do so, each suitable to particular circumstances. I have spent a good deal of my career pinning down these *species* of organizations, concluding that **there are four fundamental forms of organizations: I call them personal, programmed, professional, and project**. Figure M3.1 shows these four forms together on a diamond, two of them rather centralized, the other two rather decentralized, also two rather stable, and the other two rather dynamic in their capacity to change.

The Personal Organization (a Hub)

Let's go back to that lobster shack. It is small, but like so many small startups and even entrepreneurial organizations that grow large, everything is centered around the chief—the hub of activity. The structure of this personal organization is characterized by what it is not: elaborated. Often, everybody reports to the chief. The personal organization actually resists structure, to keep its chief free to act.

Organizations start this way because someone has to establish them and build them personally. Of course, that can be difficult to maintain when the organization grows large, but it is remarkable how many organizations keep such simple structures as long as the founder stays at the helm. And, of course, organizations that remain small will often keep using this structure simply because it's convenient to let the chief coordinate everything.

The Programmed Organization (Chains)

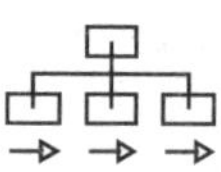

The programmed organization—namely traditional bureaucracy—favors hierarchy: the vertical chain of command that sits over the horizontal chain of operations, to control whatever possible through measures, processes, systems, and rules. Staffs of analysts, sometimes called "technocrats," design operating jobs to be as simple, specialized, and as repetitive as possible, to require a minimum of training, all for the sake of efficiency. Just as Taylor prescribed, everything possible is programmed, sometimes including the customers, so that the organization can run as smoothly as a machine. Here we find those fast-food franchises, mass production manufacturers, clerical offices in governments, and much more.

The Professional Organization (Sets)

While the programmed organization defers to the authority of office, the professional one defers to the autonomy of expertise. These are meritocracies, where highly trained professionals assemble to carry out most of their services individually, with a minimum of teamwork—to educate students in a classroom, transplant hearts in a hospital, make music in an orchestra. They may look like they are working together, but mostly they are working apart, coordinated almost automatically by their training: each knows exactly what to expect of the others. A surgeon and an anesthetist can spend hours in an operating room hardly exchanging a single word.

In the professional organization, we expect proficiency, not efficiency, let alone creativity. Imagine being wheeled into an operating room and being told by the nurse: "You have nothing to worry about: this is a really creative surgeon."

The Project Organization (Webs)

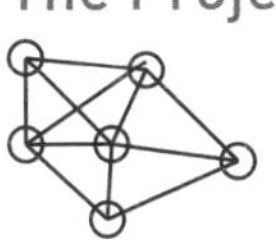

It is from the project organization that we expect creativity: these are the explorers in the world of organizations, whose experts team up to create novel outputs—crews in filmmaking, scientists in research labs. This organization violates just about every tenet of the bureaucratically best way of organizing: the structure is fluid, few procedures are formalized, unity of command gives way to matrix structure (where an expert can report to two separate managers, one on the team, the other in their specialized area of expertise). But these managers don't control so much as connect, to other teams and outsiders. Power over decision making tends to be distributed to whoever can deal with whatever is necessary at the moment.

The project organization thus becomes effective by being inefficient: its teams need slack in order to innovate. An organization cannot put blinders on its people and then expect peripheral vision.

Team Sports as Each of the Four Forms

Team sports provide wonderful examples of each of these four forms.

No sport comes close to North American football for programming, for rules, and for specialization. Standards specify who holds the ball, who catches it, who kicks it. Look at the formation on the field, not to mention the cheerleaders on the side: everybody is so neatly lined up. Even hierarchy is built right in: the quarterback calls the play and the players execute their preprogrammed moves accordingly. A sport made to measure for Taylor's scientific management!

On the other hand, can you imagine any other team sport more individualistically professional than baseball? The players stand apart, as a set, each to do their own thing. (Compare this with a huddle in football or a scrum in rugby.) No one on the field is in charge; the manager in the dugout even dresses like the players. At bat, the players come up one by one and run the bases alone. Everyone functions in a personal silo. Baseball may be the best sport to play during a pandemic.

So much of baseball is predetermined, even more than football—like those surgeons and anesthetists coordinating in an operating room. Consider the double play. The shortstop picks up the ball and flips it to the second baseman, who throws out the player at first base. The beauty is in the execution, rarely the innovation.

Hockey, basketball, rugby, and soccer—all fit the project form of organization remarkably well. When a team picks up the puck or ball at its end, it's like a new project every time: nobody quite knows how the play will proceed, the players included, who have to collaborate spontaneously to outwit their opponents. As Robert Keidel quoted a star basketball player, "Your game plan may be wiped out by what happens in the first minute of play."[16]

In any project organization, expect the unexpected. Of course, there can be surprises in the other sports too—that's the fun—but these tend to be more the exceptions. In baseball, some fans fill in a scorecard, specifying the details of every play. In hockey, who could possibly write that fast? (Soccer may be hockey in slow motion, but baseball has been described as watching the grass grow.)

In what team sport can a single individual dominate, as the chief does in a personal organization? The answer did not come easily but was obvious when it did: World Cup yacht racing. One person can get the vision, work with the designer of the boat, engage the crew, and skipper during the races. It's not that the other members of the crew are incidental; it's that their efforts revolve around that individual.

Beyond the Four, an Infinite Number of Ways to Organize

The examples above, from restaurants to sports and beyond, suggest that **many organizations fit one of the forms . . . more or less**. But no organization can fit it exactly, or, to put this differently, every organization has to incorporate some elements of the other forms—for example, some level of proficiency alongside efficiency.

The advantages of conforming to one form are harmony and consistency, as well as fit with the situation, plus clarity of structure and processes. But what if some necessary part of the organization doesn't fit that form—say a project lab in a professional hospital? Then, contamination can set in: the other parts may try to make it conform. In other words, **misfit is the weakness of the pure form**: it's tough to be a creative project in a programmed machine, maybe even tougher to be a programmed unit in a project organization.

To appreciate this, please understand that **each of the fundamental forms has a fundamental force.** *Efficiency* drives the programmed organization just as *proficiency* drives the professional organization, while *collaboration* takes central place in the project organization and *consolidation* in the personal organization. Can you imagine any organization that attends to only one of these forces and ignores the others—say, focuses on nothing but efficiency? (I'll bet you can.) **The pure form is dangerous because the organization risks flying out of control for lack of a countervailing force.**

Sure, **many organizations sensibly tilt toward one form or another, but only if they don't go over the edge.** For example, excess efficiency in a programmed organization can drive the customers as well as the workers crazy, while excessive attention to proficiency in a hospital can lead to attitudes like "The operation was a success even though the patient died." Just as a McDonald's needs creative projects for new product development, so too does a film company need a controller to keep the lid on the disorder.

Hybrids of two or more forms fit many organizations better than tilting toward a single form. I have seen a vast variety of different hybrids. For example, in a pharmaceutical company, research tends to be organized in the project form, development to test new drugs in the professional form, and manufacturing in the programmed form for efficiency.

This reinforces the conclusion that there is no one best way to organize, but many good ways to do so. I would, however, like to go farther, and suggest that **there are an infinite number of ways to organize.** That's because every one of us is unique, and it is our unique selves who make up every organization. Hence every organization has to be unique, in other words, customized to the people involved, even if only to adopt to their personal idiosyncrasies. "True, John should be reporting to Janc, but we have him reporting to Josh because he and Jane are a couple."

Three Insights to deMYTHtify the One Best Way

How much do we really understand about organizations, where we spend so much of our lives? The first Insight addresses this question, The next spoofs the programming of passengers in airplanes. And the third questions the fixation with having to be the best.

Our World of Organizations[17]

How many organizations are you connecting with today? Is ten an exaggeration? Let's start in the morning. First thing, you check your email, courtesy of a phone maker and an internet provider. Breakfast has been brought to you by farmers, factories, and food stores. Off you go to work in a business, government, or nongovernmental organization (NGO), or maybe to study in a school, transported by a bus company, unless you drive on a road patrolled by the police and maintained by the municipality. Lunch in a cafeteria could be followed by a visit to the bank or a workout at the gym. Back home, you watch the news on a TV network before reading this book, produced by a publisher. I count a lot more than ten: how many did I miss?

We live in a world of organizations, from our birth in hospitals until our burial by funeral homes. In between, we are educated, employed, entertained, and exasperated by organizations. Yet what do we really understand about them? If you want to learn about yourself, walk into a bookstore and choose from among dozens of books on self-help. If you are concerned about the economy, read any number of blogs. But between our micro selves and our macro economies, where can we go to find out how these social things called organizations really work? (Of course—to my book called *Understanding Organizations . . . Finally!* Waste no time in reading it!)

Figure M3.2 illustrates the immense variety of organizations out there, placed according to the sector in which they work: public sector governments, private sector businesses, and plural sector associations.

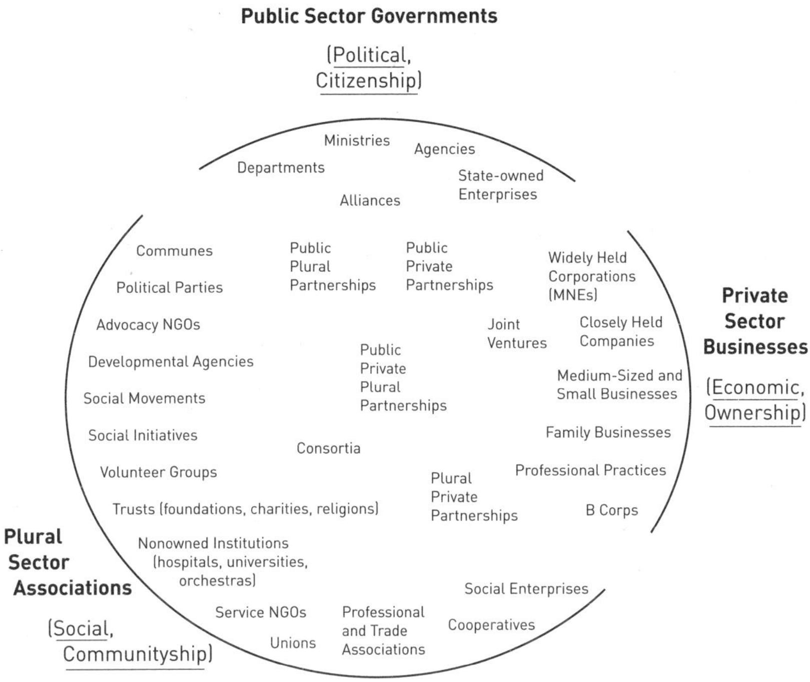

FIGURE M3.2. **Our World of Organizations**

Biggest, Boldest, Smallest, Strangest

What's the biggest organization you can think of? My choice is not quite the biggest but among the boldest. The National Health Service of England has boasted of being surpassed in size only by the Chinese Red Army, Walmart, and the Indian Railroad. Some standards for a health service! What's the smallest? How about that lobster shack by the sea? And the strangest? Try the Association of Association Executives? Or the Flying Funeral Directors of America?

Organization No-Speak

Two Canadian biologists meet. One is studying bears; the other, beavers. But let's assume they have no such vocabulary—no words for these species, just *mammal* for both, much the way we use the word *organization*.

They discuss where's the best place for a mammal to spend the winter. "In a cave, of course," says the bear biologist. To which the beaver biologist replies, "Are you kidding? They have to build a wooden structure by the side of a lake to escape their predators." "Now you're the one who's kidding," retorts the bear biologist. "Mammals don't have predators!"

They talk past each other because of the limitations of their vocabulary, just as we talk past each other because we lack vocabulary to discuss different species of organizations. Ignorance is our predator: it devours our organizations by ignoring their differences. Hermits may not need to understand organizations, but the rest of us do, especially to get past the myths about them.

Programming the Passengers

Harassed by the species bureaucracy, especially when I fly somewhere, I sought my revenge: I took notes in the thin air, and wrote a book called Why I Hate Flying, *a later version of which,* The Flying Circus, *is available on my website.*[18] *This is an excerpt.*

> I am in an airplane, so everything takes place on cue: somebody is pressing the buttons in head office. As the plane leaves the gate, a flight attendant at the front of the cabin performs some kind of ritualistic dance on cue, which everyone else ignores on cue. This is accompanied by an announcement in a language known

only to the airline people: "WelcomeaboardthisAirBlaBlaflightfromBudatoPestwithstopsinPuneandPerth. . . ."

Then the drinks come by, on cue, three pieces of ice dropped into each cup, on cue, cue, cue. "Can I have the can?" you can ask. Later, you drop a tray on cue, on which something they claim to be food is placed, which you eat obediently, on cue.

If the airplane encounters a breeze off cue, your captain is obliged to say: "We are passing through a zone of turbulence. Would you kindly return to your seats, fasten your seatbelts, and put your seatbacks back to their most uncomfortable position." (Of course, that's most likely to happen when it's finally your turn at the loo.) It is at this point that 222 clicks follow in perfect unison. You have just experienced *The Airline Salute*.

Don't get me wrong. I am not complaining that the airlines treat me like a number. Many never attain that level of individuality. I am a category, called *passenger*, worse still, *customer*. Airlines are obsessed with categories. "Jamormarmalade," "jamormarmalade," "jamormarmalade" recited an attendant to everyone as she went down the aisle like some sort of dispensing machine. And remember those categorical questions at check-in. "Have you left this bag unattended at any time since packing it?" (Yeah—it was in the trunk of my car on the way to the airport.)

There is a special word for organizations obsessed with categories: *bureaucracy*. Bureaucracy is not about tape that is red or people who sit on their butts. It's about categories. Airlines are the most categorizing organizations off the face of the earth.

If you read the airline magazines, you know that those Great Gurus of Management have declared bureaucracy dead. We live in the age of turbulence; they keep telling us. Actually, I haven't noticed. Things seem pretty calm up here in the sky, pretty calmly categorical. Bureaucracy is doing just fine in the thin air.

The Best Is Too Low a Standard[19]

In our search for getting better, we can get past having to be the best.

Sylvie Bernier won the gold medal in three-meter springboard diving at the Olympic Games in Los Angeles in 1984. She was up against severe competition: a heavily favored diver from California whose mother had won back-to-back diving double Olympic gold medals in succession (1952, 1956) in the three-meter springboard and ten-meter platform events.

I got to know Sylvie as a participant in McGill's International Masters for Health Leadership Program. When I asked her what distinguishes people who attain such success, she told me an extraordinary story—not about being the best, but about being herself.

Sylvie was twenty at the time, and on her own—a Québécoise from the farthest corner of the continent, competing against a popular local. Or at least she made herself alone. When she got to the finals, she blocked off everyone and everything: her coach, her family, friends, journalists, reports on radio and TV—anything that could possibly tell her how she was doing, so that she could concentrate on her personal effort. Sure, she wanted to win—that's in the nature of the event—but this was not how she got there.

When she left that springboard for the last dive, Sylvie did not know whether she was going for gold or already relegated to less. But that didn't matter, because she was competing against herself: to dive as well as she possibly could.

What does being the best mean anyway? The Olympics may keep score, but is Mozart better than Beethoven? How about Édith Piaf—was she the best? Who knows? But was she ever good! Indeed, she was incomparable, thus in less danger of being labeled the best.

So, let's drop, not our standards, but our obsession: never set out to be the best. It's too low a standard. Set out to be good, as good as you can possibly be. Do *your* best.

III Three Myths of Managing

Myth 4	**Management is a profession that relies on the evidence of analysis.**

deMyth 4	**Managing is a practice that is grounded in the experience of life.**

Evidence-based medicine has become very fashionable in that profession, and from there the idea has spread to other fields. Yet when I have asked groups of physicians about the extent to which they use evidence compared with experience, they have come out all over the map. We might expect psychiatrists to make extensive use of experience, but even some surgeons have claimed that experience is no less important in their practice than evidence.

To appreciate the difference between evidence and experience, consider this little story. On the right side of the handlebar of a bicycle, you can find a little number—let's say 4—which tells you which gear the back wheel is in. This is evidence. Experience is what you live while cycling in that gear—perhaps that the pedals are going around too quickly for the terrain you are on. **Evidence is what we figure; experience is what we feel.**

Effective managers use evidence when they can but mostly they rely far more on experience. This is why management is neither a profession nor a science. Observe managers at work, as I have done in two studies—of five chief executives for a week each and twenty-nine managers of all kinds for a day each—and this quickly becomes apparent, as we shall see in examples that follow.

Management Is Not a Profession

For years, I went around asking groups of people in this job: "What happened the day you became a manager? Were you offered any guidance at all?" The response was almost always the same: puzzled looks, then shrugs. Mostly, you are supposed to figure this out for yourself, like sex, I suppose, often with similarly embarrassing consequences. Yesterday you were playing the drums; today you find yourself managing people who are making music. Everything has changed, yet you are on your own, confused and overwhelmed. These are hardly the hallmarks of a profession.

Linda Hill wrote a great book about *Becoming a Manager.*[20] Here is the comment of one manager: "I didn't have the slightest idea what my job was. I walked in giggling and laughing because I had been promoted and had no idea what principles or styles to be guided by. After the first day I felt like I had run into a brick wall."

Management Is Not a Science

Science is about the development of systematic knowledge through research. Management schools do much research, but surprisingly little of it has anything to do with the management process itself. It's mostly about the business functions, and especially how they use the scientific disciplines—for example, economics in finance and psychology in marketing. Many business schools barely even teach management—perhaps because they are so busy teaching leadership.

Medicine and engineering do apply considerable science, codified and certified as to its effectiveness. That is what makes them professions, which means that their students can be taught the relevant skills before entering practice, independent of the context where they will practice. Such professionals can therefore carry their skills from one context to another—say, from one operating room to the next. Managers can hardly do that; indeed, it takes even an experienced manager a good deal of time to figure out what's going on in a new job, and then how to proceed. In contrast, give physicians an operating room with the necessary staff and equipment, and off they go, almost immediately.

Not only is there no certification to practice management, but some of the best managers have never spent a day in a business school classroom, and we have suspicions (discussed in Myth 5) about many others who spent a year or two there. Should we bemoan this? No, we should celebrate management as a practice, embedded in everyday living, rather than being removed from it.

Management Is a Practice

As illustrated in the triangle in Figure M4.1, **management happens where the experience of craft meets the evidence of science, enlightened by the insights of art.** Art is about insight, vision is intuitive; it's idea based. Craft is practical, engaging; it's experience based. And science is factual and analytical: it's evidence based.

As noted, compared with professionals, managers can't rely on much evidence from science, although they can certainly make use of analysis, within reason. And their use of art depends on their own personality: some, especially entrepreneurs, can be highly creative, while others are hardly so, yet can be successful, nonetheless. Craft, in contrast, is fundamental in the practice of managing, which is another way of saying that experience is key, not only about managing itself, but also in knowing the industry and the organization where it is practiced. (This is what makes the notion of a guest manager so oxymoronic, other than by a conductor during a concert.) People who see themselves as professional managers who can manage anything all too often prove capable of managing nothing. (See "Enough of MORE. We Need Better" on MythSite.org/more.)

This is not to say that managers don't tilt on the triangle. Entrepreneurs, as noted, tend to be strong on the art, hence many are called "visionaries." These days, too many others tilt toward the science, at least in the form of analysis, including those lofty leaders who deem performance targets from above. (We discuss the excessive use of analysis in Myths 7, 8, and 9.) Of course, experience that excludes evidence is likewise excessive, as is art that excludes both evidence and experience.

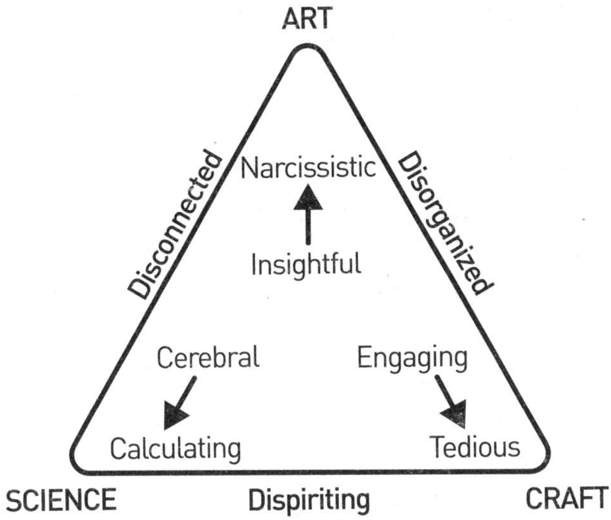

FIGURE M4.1. **Managing as a Practice: Where Art, Craft, and Science Meet**

Thus, the three corners of the triangle of Figure M4.1 are perilous places for managers to be. As shown, too much science in the form of analysis leads to a *calculating* style of managing, where relationships become dehumanized, while too much art can lead to a *narcissistic* style of managing—art for the sake of the artist. And too much craft can be *tedious*, as managers hesitate to venture beyond their own experience.

Effective managing thus happens within the triangle, shown there by three common styles. *Insightful management*—visionary and intuitive—is commonly found in the personal organization (discussed in Myth 3): closest to art but restrained with some attention to craft and/or science. *Cerebral management*, deliberate and analytical, is shown closest to science, but tempered with some attention to art and/or craft. Look for it especially in the programmed organization. And *engaging management*, hands-on and helpful, is mostly craft, but supported by some art and constrained by some science. We might look for this especially in the project form of organization—but not only, if communityship is as important as I suggest in Myth 2. In this regard, compare nursing, which is concerned with continuous care, with medicine, which is more about interventionist cure. Might nursing, as a consequence, make for a better predisposition to managing than medicine?

To conclude, **put together a good deal of craft with the right touch of art, alongside an appropriate use of analysis, and you end up with the practice that is managing.**

Two Insights to deMYTHtify Professional Management

The first Insight offers some stories of management as a practice. And the second enables you to position yourself on the art/craft/science triangle.

Some Stories of Management as a Practice[21]

A few good stories can bring the experience of managing to life.

Abbas Gullet managed the Red Cross Delegation for the refugee camps in Ngara, Tanzania, that housed many Hutus who had escaped from the war in Rwanda. This was no easy job—he had to make sure everything was under control so that the place would not blow apart from some unfortunate event. In the midst of this came news that a boat had overturned on

Lake Victoria, causing almost a thousand deaths. Realizing that they might be the closest Red Cross delegation, Abbas collected a number of his staff, grabbed some supplies—body bags, stretchers, disinfectant—and headed there by road, arriving one day after the accident, the first NGO on site. They stayed two weeks, working long hours arranging for body recovery, setting up a morgue in a nearby stadium, and helping the grieving families.

Alan Whelan was Sales Manager for Global Computing and Electronics at a British telecommunications company, so you might think he'd be meeting customers, or at least working with his people to help them sell to customers. When I observed him, Alan was selling, all right, but to an executive of his own company, who was reluctant to sign off on his biggest contract.

As managing director of Hawkshead Communications in the UK, Carol Haslam had to put together projects across TV networks, around the world, while pitching ideas to her potential clients and convincing them of her firm's ability to execute them.

Art, Craft, Science: Who Do You Think You Are?

How do you see yourself, as a manager, or otherwise—as an artist, a craftsperson, or oriented to science and analysis? Table M4.1 lists various words across three columns, down ten rows. Beverly Patwell, an organization development consultant, and I developed this to help people consider themselves, or others they know, as inclined to favor art, craft, and/or science.

On a paper copy or an electronic screen, in each of the ten rows, circle or highlight one of the three entries in each row that best describes how you see yourself. Just one entry on each line,

TABLE M4.1. **Who Are You?**

ART	CRAFT	SCIENCE
Ideas	Experiences	Facts
Intuitive	Practical	Analytical
Heart	Hands	Head
Strategies	Processes	Outcomes
Inspiring	Engaging	Informing
Passionate	Helpful	Reliable
Novel	Realistic	Determined
Imagining	Learning	Organizing
Seeing It	Doing It	Thinking It
"The possibilities are endless!"	"Consider it done!"	"That's perfect!"
Count:	**Count:**	**Count:**

please—the first thing that comes to your mind. Then add up the number of choices down each of the three columns, and put the totals at the bottom. Together, they should add up to ten.

The first column gives your score for art, the second for craft, the third for science. Now go to the triangle in Figure M4.2, and identify the horizontal line labeled A (for art) that corresponds to your score in the first column. Then do the same for your score in the second column on the diagonal line marked C (for craft). Where these two lines meet (shown in the example on the upper left as 7 for A, and 2 for C) should also be where your score falls on the S line (for science), to make a total of ten (hence S1 in this example). If it doesn't, you have probably scored low on science!

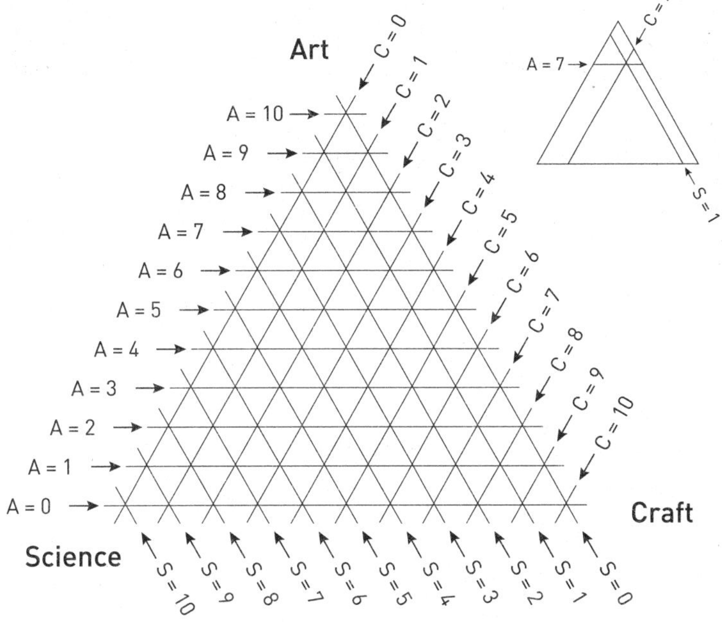

FIGURE M4.2. **Positioning Yourself**

This place on the triangle is how you see yourself with regard to practicing art, craft, and science. Bear in mind that these are your own perceptions; other people may see you differently. You might even see yourself differently if you were in a different job, or living the life you dream of. If you work in a team, or live in a family, it can be revealing to have everyone do this for themselves and then for each other, to compare the results.

While a variety of scores can be found in most organizations, sometimes the people do tilt one way or another—perhaps art in advertising agencies, craft in engineering offices, science as analysis in accounting firms. Nevertheless, all organizations need people everywhere on the triangle to maintain balance.

Myth 5 MBA education prepares students to manage.

deMyth 5 MBA education distorts the practice of management; development programs that use managers' experience enhance it.

You are a manager who is performing well, but intent on performing better. Should you do an MBA? Not if it's about the administration of business rather than the practice of managing. Will sitting in nice, neat rows listening to lectures about business functions, plus pronouncing case study strategies for companies you know little about, really make you a better manager?[22]

This myth follows from the last. Were management a profession, then managers, like physicians, would have to be formally educated before they could be allowed to practice. They would be taught the evidence of science, and trained in the imperatives of analysis. But since management is a practice, grounded in the experience of craft, this kind of training can distort the practice. **Excessive attention to analysis distances the education from whatever experience the participants may have, and thus encourages macro-leading.**

For years, I went around giving talks at business schools about what is wrong with **conventional MBA education for management**, namely that it **trains the wrong people in the wrong ways with the wrong consequences.** Don't get me wrong: many MBA programs do a fine job of developing business specialists, such as financial analysts and marketing researchers.

They just need to stop confounding this with the practice of managing. There is plenty of business education in the business schools, but hardly any management education.

Let's consider the wrong people in the wrong ways, and then the wrong consequences, before suggesting how the right people can be developed in better ways with beneficial consequences.

Wrong People in the Wrong Ways

A manager can no more be created in a classroom than can a swimmer. Both need to be immersed in the reality, not just to understand it, but to experience it. Taking young people with little or no managerial experience and graduating them as ready to manage is an affront to society—as legions of people subjected to such managers can attest. (The Harvard Business School has long made similar claims about leadership, at one point stating on its website that it is "focused on one purpose—developing leaders." Can a leader really be developed in a classroom?)

This leads to the wrong ways. We can't teach the art of managing—it's innate, if present at all. Nor can we enhance the craft of managing when experience is absent, or ignored. This leaves the science, or at least applied science in the form of analysis. So, here is where MBA programs concentrate their attention: on teaching technique, in the form of analysis, alongside theory, especially in the business functions of finance, marketing, accounting, and more.

The problem with this is that **the functions of business are not the practice of managing**. Sure, managers, particularly in business, need to understand these functions. But they also need to understand a lot more than that, as we shall discuss in the next myth. You might think that this would be particularly evident in so-called Executive MBA programs, that at least take the right people, that is, many with managerial experience. But mostly, they teach them in the same way. For years, one top-rated business school claimed on its website that "The Wharton Executive MBA program is a true MBA program," whose students "cover the same curriculum and... complete the same coursework... the only difference is how it is delivered and the high level of experience of students." How extraordinary: boasting about doing no more for experienced managers than for people who have never managed!

Is the teaching of cases, popularized by Harvard, any different? You might think so—after all, cases are designed to bring experience into the classroom. But what kind of experience is this? Sterling Livingston, a Harvard professor after having functioned in the world of management, published a famous article in the *Harvard Business Review* entitled the "Myth of the Well-Educated Manager."[23] He questioned the "second-handedness" of such education, instead of enabling students to "learn from their own firsthand experience.... They study written case histories that describe problems or opportunities, discovered by someone else, which they discuss, but do nothing about." This "overdevelops an individual's analytical ability" while leaving their "ability to take action and to get things done underdeveloped."

But Livingston had one thing wrong. The problem goes far beyond second-handedness. First, Harvard cases "exaggerate the role of individual leaders. Sixty-two percent of cases feature heroic managers acting alone,"[24] as if the CEO is the main source of what actually went on.

Second, these cases tend to be researched by assistants, who give their report to a professor, who writes or edits the case, which is then used by other professors, with students whose knowledge of the company is restricted to the few pages they read the day before the class. There, they must pronounce on what the company—often the CEO—should do. I count this as about fifth-handed. Such cases may be fine for illustrating some point in marketing, but what kind of managers do they develop? (See the Insight below entitled "Jack's Turn.")

The Harvard executive education programs ran an ad in *The Economist* some years ago showing an executive-looking woman effusing: "We studied four companies a day. This isn't theory. This is experience." This is nonsense.

Case study teaching gives MBAs the impression that, based on analyzing hundreds of cases, they have been taught to make managerial decisions. Maybe they have been taught to speak a good game, which helps them get ahead in a fast-moving world. Similarly, in MBA programs that concentrate on theory more than cases, students graduate with a vocabulary that sounds good in a world of one best ways. The trouble with all this is that, **while the business schools barely teach management, they graduate people believing they can manage anything.** Does learning how to market fast-moving consumer goods, conduct competitive analysis of industries, and use algorithms to raise capital in financial markets prepare graduates to manage a hospital or an NGO, let alone a balanced business?

In her book, *Becoming a Manager,* Linda Hill cites a study in which almost two-thirds of the graduates of business education reported "that they used their MBA skills marginally or not at all in their first management assignments"—precisely where such skills should be most helpful.[25]

She concluded from her own research that "the education many business schools provide does little to prepare managers for their day-to-day realities."

Wrong Consequences

All of this results in consequences that are wrong for organizations and society. Imagine if, upon graduation, MBAs were stamped on their forehead with a skull and crossbones that read: "Warning! Not prepared to manage." Instead, for starters, the MBA degree confers on many of them an undeserved headstart in management, by enabling them to parachute into managerial positions a slab or two above the base of the organization, so they never get to function where it makes its products or renders its services. How better to set them on the road to lofty leadership—often paved by an old boy's network of graduates from the same school already in positions of senior management?

A faster way to the top, out of the prestigious MBA programs, is to begin in a prominent consulting firm, make a reputation by hopping from one client analysis to another, then to parachute straight into some CEO chair—usually in a publicly traded corporation driven by the short-term demands of the financial markets, but sometimes even a hospital or an NGO whose board of businesspeople is intent on having it run like a business.

As the MBA has become more fashionable, even managers without the degree have been inclined to adopt its approach to managing: detached, analytic, numeric, centralized. They become the new bureaucrats. And this exacerbates the hierarchical divide in the organization, between the managers and the managed, which, in turn, exacerbates the class divides that have become so prevalent in the world today.[26]

Put differently, thanks in good part to the MBA credential, "business class" has become more than a place on an airplane. **Do we really want a society of elitist "leaders" trained in analysis and promoted on fast tracks apart from the everyday work of organizations?**

All of this would hardly matter if these managers did well. Indeed, business schools boast about how many of their graduates become CEOs. But how about their performance once there? This is something these centers of research hardly research. But the little evidence we do have is startling, as discussed in an Insight at the end of this Myth.

Developing Managers Naturally

Beyond business education can be management education that develops managers by letting their experience do much of the talking. Such *social learning* starts with the right people, namely managers who have grounded experience in the practice, normally in one organization or at least one industry. In the classroom, sure, we faculty have our theories, techniques, and other ideas to teach. But they take on meaning when seasoned managers are given the opportunity to reflect on them in terms of their own experience and share the resulting insights with each other. T.S. Eliot wrote in one of his poems "We had the experience but missed the meaning." Management education should be about getting the meaning. In a classroom designed to do that, it is quite remarkable how effective that can be.

We have all heard the calls for management education to be more realistic, more practical. **Managers hardly need an educational setting to be more practical—they live practice every day. They need it to becomemore thoughtful.** Education, by its very nature, should be hands *off*, to enable the learners to step back and suspend their beliefs so that they can develop more effective beliefs.

We have carried these ideas forward in a family of programs for mastering the practice of management, each intended to shift business education to management education combined with management development—this, to *do* a better job, not just *get* a better job. We began with the International Masters Program for Managers (impm.org), which ran for twenty-five years as a partnership of five universities around the world, each doing a ten-day module. This was followed by the International Masters for Health Leadership (mcgill.ca/imhl), and then the McGill-HEC EMBA, as well as various shorter programs, some designed for particular organizations. Another program, CoachingOurselves.com, was established to bring this form of management development to small groups of managers within their own organizations: no faculty, no facilitator, no coach, just managers learning from each other by downloading and discussing topics such as "Dealing with the Pressure of Managing" and "Developing Our Organization as a Community."

Each degree program welcomes experienced people into modules of several days, so that they can remain in the jobs, where they get the experience that feeds into the classroom. These modules are devoted, not to the business functions, but to five managerial mindsets: the *reflective mindset,* the *action mindset*, the *collaborative mindset*, the *analytical mindset*, and what we call the *worldly mindset* (rather than the global mindset, about the context of the organization).[27]

In the classroom, the managers sit at small round tables in a flat room so that they can go in and out of workshops at a moment's notice—no need to "break out," or remain isolated in an educational silo, as in those sloped U-shaped classrooms. A fifty-fifty rule calls for half the class time to be devoted to these workshops, where the managers reflect on their experience and share their insights with each other. Hence the learning is customized to the needs of each manager.

This design has stimulated a number of other innovations in the classroom and beyond, such as novel seating arrangements, including *keynote listeners* who sit with their backs to the table and then report out in plenary *fishbowl conversations.*[28] *Friendly consulting* enables managers to seek advice from their colleagues (in a sense, living cases). Likewise, in the *managerial exchanges,* each manager spends several days with a colleague at his or her workplace to broaden their mutual understanding of the practice of managing.

It has been said never to send a changed person back to an unchanged organization. Yet almost all management education and development programs do just that. Hence, in some of our programs, we ask each manager to develop an *impact team* of colleagues or reports back at work, to carry their learning into their own organization, so that others can benefit too.

To conclude this discussion, **the MBA is fine so long as it is recognized for what it does well, namely train people for certain specialized jobs in business. But it must also be**

recognized for what it does badly, namely train people to manage. We need *management* education, as development.

Two Insights to deMTYHtify the MBA

We begin with a not-so-apocryphal story of a Harvard MBA student who takes the school's dictates at its word, and follow with some surprising evidence about how MBAs perform as CEOs.

Jack's Turn[29]

In lecture courses, students are waiting for you to give "the answer." There's a built-in bias against action. What we say with the case method is "Look, I know you don't have enough information—but given the information you do have, what are you going to do?"[30]

"OK, Jack, here you are at Mammoth Inc. What should the company do now?"

The professor and eighty or so of Jack's classmates anxiously await his reply to the "cold call." Jack is prepared; he has thought about this ever since he was told that the case study method is intended to "challenge conventional thinking." He has also been reminded repeatedly that since good managers are decisive, good MBA students have to take a stand. So, Jack swallows hard and answers the question.

"How can I answer the question?" Jack begins. He continues: "I barely heard of Mammoth before yesterday. Yet today you want me to pronounce on its strategy. Yesterday, I had two other cases to prepare. So Mammoth, with so many employees and products, got a couple of hours. I read the case over once quickly, and again, um, less quickly. I never knowingly used any of Mammoth's products. (I didn't even know that the company makes the rat poison I use in my basement.) I never went inside any of its factories. I've never even been to Come by Chance, Newfoundland, where Mammoth is headquartered. I spoke to none of its customers (except myself), let alone any of the people mentioned in the case. Besides, this is a pretty high-tech company and I'm a pretty low-tech guy. My work experience, such as it was, took place in a furniture factory. All I have to go by are these few pages. This is a superficial exercise. I refuse to answer your question."

What happens to Jack? At the business school, I'll let you guess. But from there, he goes back to the furniture business, where he immerses himself in the products and the processes, the people and the industry. With no head start from any old boy, but his courage to be decisive and challenge conventional thinking, Jack rises to head up the place. Here, with hardly any industry analysis at all (that would have come in a later course), he and his people learn their way to a strategy that transforms the industry.

Back in that class, the professor turns to Bill, sitting next to Jack, who leaps in. He, too, has never been to Come by Chance, but that hardly stops him. He makes a clever point or two and eventually gets that MBA. This gets him into a prestigious consulting firm, where, as in those case study classes, he leaps from one organization to another, each time making a clever point or two, concerning issues he recently knew nothing about, always leaving before implementation begins.

As this kind of experience pours in, it is not long before Bill becomes chief executive of a major appliance company. (He never consulted for one, but it does get him thinking about that Mammoth case.) There, after downsizing a few thousand of its human resources, he formulates a glitzy high-tech strategy which is implemented through a dramatic program of acquisitions. What happens to that I'll let you guess again.

"Readers [of the book What They Really Teach You at the Harvard Business School] *are probably asking, Read the case and do that analysis in two to four hours? Harvard's answer is yes. Students need to prepare two to three cases each day.... So students must work toward getting their analysis done fast as well as done well."*[31]

Read on.

MBAs as CEOs: Some Surprising Evidence[32]

Business schools like to boast about how many of their graduates have become CEOs. But how do these people do as CEOs? What little evidence we have is rather surprising.

MBA students enter the prestigious business schools smart, determined, and often aggressive. Case studies teach them how to pronounce cleverly on situations they know little about, while analytic techniques give them the impression that they can tackle any problem—no in-depth experience necessary. With graduation comes the confidence of having been to a proper business school, not to mention the "old boys" network that can boost them to the "top." Then what?

A decade after its publication in 1990, Joseph Lampel and I looked at a book called *Inside the Harvard Business School*, by David Ewing, long an insider.[33]

It listed nineteen Harvard alumni who "had made it to the top." Our attention was drawn to a few of them who would not have been on that list much later. So, we studied the post-1990 record of all nineteen.[34]

How did they do? In a word, badly. A majority, ten, seemed clearly to have failed, meaning that their company went bankrupt, they were forced out of office, a major merger backfired, and so on. The performance of another four we found to be questionable. Some of these fourteen CEOs built up or turned around businesses, prominently and dramatically, only to see them weaken or collapse just as dramatically. Five did seem to do well.

Of course, a couple of years in a classroom does not necessarily destroy one's potential for management—there were, after all, those five. But the performance of the fourteen suggests either that this business school has succeeded in putting some wrong people on the track to that top, or else that its emphasis on cases may have given some right people the wrong impression of managing.

These results were published prominently (including in an article in *Fortune* magazine and also in my book *Managers Not MBAs*). While they did not prove anything, one might think that they should have set off an alarm bell or two. Nope.

Later, two other business school professors weighed in.[35] One was my first doctoral student, Danny Miller, the other, Xiaowei Xu. They authored two articles with much larger samples and more troubling results. In one, using an ingenious sample of 444 chief executives of American corporations celebrated on the covers of *Business Week*, *Fortune*, and *Forbes* magazines from 1970 to 2008, they compared the subsequent performance of those companies that were headed by MBAs—one quarter of the total—with the ones that were not.

Both sets of companies declined in performance after those cover stories (Miller commented later that "it's hard to stay on top"), but the ones headed by MBAs declined more quickly, and this "performance gap remained significant even seven years after the cover story appeared." Yet the compensation of the MBA CEOs increased, indeed about 15 percent faster than the others!

The second study used a wider sample: 5004 CEOs of major US public corporations. The results were much the same: "MBA CEOs are more apt than their non-MBA counterparts to engage in short-term strategic expedients such as positive earnings management and suppression of R&D, which in turn are followed by compromised firm market valuations." Once again, these MBA CEOs were rewarded for this "performance."

So why do the business schools persist in their claims about leadership that could be producing mismanagement? The answer is too obvious: with so many of their graduates getting to the "top," why change, especially given the fees they can charge for this education?

Myth 6 Managers plan, organize, coordinate, and control (i.e., they control, control, control, and control).

deMyth 6 Managers struggle to control their own jobs, which entails communicating more than controlling, linking as much as leading, dealing as well as doing.

In 1916, Henri Fayol, head of a French mining company, introduced this vocabulary to describe managerial work: four words for *controlling.*[36] (Fayol actually included a fifth—*commanding*—yet another word for *controlling.*) His vocabulary remains prevalent to the present day. No wonder so many managers are called control freaks.

Watch a manager at work, or yourself as a manager, and try to relate what you are seeing with these words. When a company CEO meets a government official, are they controlling, let alone planning, organizing, or coordinating? How about when they present a plaque to a retiring employee? Or return from a conference to tell a colleague about a conversation with a customer?

My doctoral thesis, way back when, was based on the observation of five chief executives for a week each—in three businesses, a hospital, and a school system. I challenged these words as insufficient to describe the roles that I saw these managers performing, also that these words suggested a distorted image of the characteristics of managerial work—as calm and collected. These conclusions were published in my first book, *The Nature of Managerial Work*, and in an award-winning *Harvard Business Review* article, "The Manager's Job: Folklore and Fact."[37] Later, I developed them further in a book called *Managing* (subsequently distilled as *Simply Managing*), based on observing twenty-nine managers of all kinds for a day each. Nevertheless, the myth of the manager as controlling and being in control persists.

> I spent a day with Bramwell Tovey, conductor of the Winnipeg Symphony Orchestra, mostly in rehearsal.[38] I asked him about being in charge. "You have to subordinate yourself to the composer," he replied. So, does the director of an orchestra actually *direct* the orchestra, namely *control* its musicians? His reply was "We never talk about the relationship!"

The Characteristics of Managerial Work

The characteristics that I observed in my research—the pace of the work, the pressures, the interruptions, and more—suggest, not control at all, but quite the opposite: that **managers struggle to keep control of their own jobs.**

The Pressures and the Pace

The manager as systematic planner is pure myth, even about planning their own work. The overwhelming evidence points to managerial work as proceeding at an unrelenting, and often unpredictable, pace, from foremen's activities averaging forty-eight seconds long to half the activities of the five chief executives I observed lasting less than nine minutes.[39] "[E]xecutives just sort of dash around all the time," as a group of researchers put it.[40] The chief executives I observed met a steady stream of callers, from their arrival in the morning until their departure in the evening, with coffee breaks and lunches inevitably work related. As one put it to me, his work is "one damn thing after another." Here is an example from the day I observed the head nurse of a surgical ward:

> Fabienne Lavoie was working from 7:20 a.m. to 6:45 p.m. at a pace that exhausted me as an observer. At one point, in the space of a few minutes, she discussed a dressing with a surgeon, put through a patient's hospital card, rearranged her schedule board, spoke with someone in reception, checked on a patient who had a fever, made a call to fill in a vacancy, discussed some medication, and chatted with a patient's relative.[41]

Why such a pace? One reason is the inherently open-ended nature of the job. Managers are held responsible for the success of what they manage, yet have no tangible mileposts to stop and say, "Now my job is finished, even for now." **The manager has to keep going, never knowing when success is truly assured, or else when things might suddenly come crashing down.**

Fragmentation and Interruption

Most work in society involves specialization and concentration. An engineer can spend months designing a bridge. Not so with managing. It is fragmented and constantly interrupted. Someone calls about a fire in a facility; next a few emails are scanned, then an assistant appears to inform about a legal challenge from a consumer group. Surprising, too, is that significant activities are interspersed with mundane ones in no particular pattern. Swedish economist Sune Carlson, who studied nine Swedish managing directors, having found such interruption, asked why they didn't make better use of their secretaries.[42] But I observed managers who actually encouraged interruption, perhaps to ensure the flow of current information, also because, **no matter what they are doing, managers are plagued by what they *might* do and what they *must* do.** Plus, with the hectic pace, maybe they just get bored easily when things slow.

> Harry Henschel, CEO of the Bulova Watch Company, had a big office, but placed his desk so he looked down a corridor. When working alone, with the door open, he sometimes waved passers-by in to have a chat.

Orientation to Action

The pattern, pace, and pressures of managing do not encourage the development of reflective planners. Rather, the job breeds adaptive information manipulators who prefer live, concrete action—dynamic, current, non-routine. "I don't want it good; I want it Tuesday," said a manager. Sudden information can get top priority, interrupting meetings, rearranging agendas, and evoking flurries of activity. As a consequence, **superficiality is an occupational hazard of managerial work. To succeed, managers have to become proficient at their superficiality.**

It has been said that an expert is someone who knows more and more about less and less until finally they know everything about nothing. The manager's problem is the opposite: knowing less and less about more and more until finally they know nothing about everything. Imagine what happens when the expert meets the manager. (They did, before the Boeing 737 and NASA *Challenger* tragedies.)

Oral Communication

Studies have been consistent in their finding that managing is about talking and listening a lot more than reading and writing. As Jeanne Liedtka, professor at the Darden School, has put it, **"Talk is the technology of leadership."**

Moreover, I found in my research that **managers cherish soft information.** Gossip, hearsay, and speculation form a good part of their information diet. The reason appears to be its timeliness: today's gossip can be tomorrow's fact. But by then, it may be too late. To quote one manager, "I would be in trouble if the accounting reports held information I did not already have."[43]

Moreover, while "hard" formal information may seem to be definitive, soft, informal information can be much richer, even if less reliable. In meetings, for example, there are facial expressions, tones of voice, gestures. Accordingly, **the strategic data bank of an organization can be found at least as much in the heads of its managers as in the files of its computers.**

Lateral Contacts

There is no hint in Fayol's words of the extent to which managerial work happens with people outside the manager's unit, whom they do not control. But there is plenty of evidence in the research. Typically, managers of all kinds spend an awful lot of their time, often half or more, interacting with such people—customers, suppliers, partners, and other stakeholders, as well as colleagues in their own organization—as they do with the people who report directly to them

Someone once described the manager as that person who sees the visitors so that everyone else can get their work done. After observing Brian Adams, a program manager for a new aircraft at Canadair, I described his job as lateral management with a vengeance. He had enormous responsibility, yet not a great deal of formal authority over many of the people with whom he had to work in their "partner" organizations (subcontractors, responsible for parts of the aircraft). Likewise, Charlie Zinkan, who ran the Banff National Park, sat between all sorts of interests—developers, environmentalists, others—to whom he had to respond, often as delicately as possible.

Add these characteristics together and you get a picture of managing, less about controlling, and more about being controlled. Shortly after my "Folklore and Fact" article was published, an article about it in the *New York Times* described **managing as "calculated chaos" and "controlled disorder."** Indeed!

None of these characteristics could have come as a surprise to anyone who has ever spent a day in a managerial office, doing the job or watching it. Yet this struck a chord, especially with managers themselves. Time and again, they told me, "You make me feel so good! While I thought that all those other managers were planning, organizing, coordinating, and controlling, I was consistently trying to keep the lid on all the chaos." Bear in mind: all this *is* managing—normal managing.

Span of Control?

Lyndall Urwick, who followed Fayol with his own collection of words for controlling,[44] claimed famously in 1956 that "No supervisor can supervise directly the work of more than five or, at the most, six subordinates, whose work interlocks."[45] Go tell that to the hundred or so musicians who play together with a single conductor, or a like number of workers in a factory who report to a single foreman. Even to a research team that prefers fewer than five members, for the sake of easy communication.

What's going on? A lot more than controlling! Sure, work that interlocks can be coordinated by a manager who uses direct supervision, namely giving direct orders to people. But there are other ways to coordinate work in organizations. In the symphony orchestra, a professional organization, coordination is achieved not by the waving of that wand so much as by the fact that each musician knows exactly what to expect of the others. In an assembly plant, it's by everyone's job being so programmed. No need for the foreman to tell the workers what to do. As for project teams, the members coordinate by mutual adjustment, meaning straightforward conversation, which is why even five members can sometimes be too many. Each team has a manager, but more to connect than to control—for example, to liaise with other teams.

So, what else do managers do beside controlling?

The Roles of Managing

Henri Fayol claimed that managers control; Warren Bennis, that they lead; Tom Peters, that they do ("Don't think, do" is the phrase I favor). All are wrong apart, but all are right together: every manager has to do all of this, and more. On Wall Street, of course, managers do deals. And let's not forget all that communicating, especially with outsiders, meaning that managers also link.

The reality of this job is that managers *communicate* more than they *control,* they *link* as much as they *lead, and* they *deal* as well as they *do.* These are six basic roles of managerial work. Managers have to engage themselves in all of them, even if their situation can drive them to favor one or another. But **overemphasizing any one role can drive managing over the edge**. Controlling is heavy—too much of it can weigh the place down—while *doing* can be light. Too much of that and the organization can fly off in all directions. Likewise, fixation on leading can distract managers from managing, while fixating on linking to outsiders can reduce the job to public relations. The managers who only communicate never get anything done, while those who must *do* everything themselves can end up doing it all alone.

Figure M6.1 thus shows the manager as sitting between the unit managed and the rest of the organization, surrounded by the outside world, with these six roles shown on three planes, labelled *information*, *people*, and *action*. On the action plane, managers influence action directly, by doing and dealing. One level back, on the people plane, they do so indirectly, by leading and linking; and two levels back, on the information plane, they do so by communicating and controlling.

> On the day of observation, Carol Haslam, of Hawkshead Communications, could be seen working on all three plains. On the action plane, she was deeply involved with developing projects for new films—she was doing deals galore. On the people plane, she was using her vast network of contacts to promote these

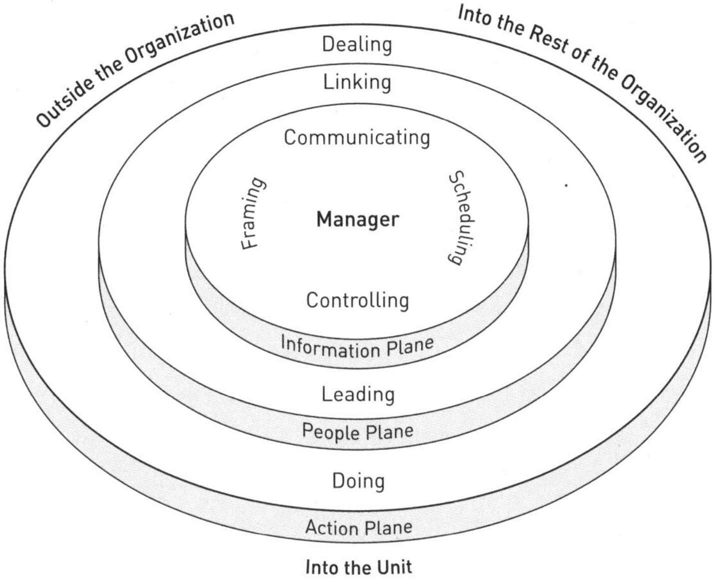

FIGURE M6.1. **A Model of Managing**

projects, as well as building teams of filmmakers to make them. And on the information plane, all day long she was collecting and disseminating ideas, data, and advice.

Let's go over all six roles, one by one, with examples from my research.

Communicating All Around, on the Information Plane

Watch a manager at work, and one thing readily becomes apparent: the great amount of time they spend simply communicating—especially by talking, and the best of them, by listening. Study after study, of all kinds of managers, has demonstrated that they spend upwards of half their time simply communicating, with all kinds of people, inside and outside their unit. Much of the time, they simply gather information to get informed, and disseminate some of it to others, to ensure it gets to the right place.

> I observed this communicating, intertwined with leading, especially on the day I spent with Stephen Omollo, operating manager of a Red Cross refugee camp in Ngara, Tanzania. As he walked through the camps, he used every means possible to sense what was going on, greeting everyone he passed, smiling and laughing. "My job is to assist and train the local staff," Stephen said, "but there is a need to tour on foot. You need to laugh with the people."

Controlling Inside, on the Information Plane

Managers do control, although usually less than implied in the traditional literature. They exercise their formal authority by issuing orders, setting targets, and assigning responsibilities. Much of this comes under the label of *resource allocation*, namely, to determine how money, time, material, and work are distributed across the unit.

> In the refugee camps of Ngara, controlling was front and center, because everything had to be kept under tight wraps, for fear of a small incident blowing into a major crisis. "You just need to put your ear to the ground, Stephen, and find out more about what the feelings are among the refugees," Abbas Gullet, in charge of the Red Cross Delegation, told Stephen, his report, at a meeting in the compound. Reinforcing this control were the many Red Cross systems, procedures, rules and regulations.

Leading Inside, on the People Plane

Here is where leading comes in, not on top of managing, but as one of its essential roles. Managers coach, nurture, and inspire the individuals who report to them; they develop and strengthen the teams that are made up of these people; and across the entire organization, they help to establish and maintain its culture.

I observed Norm Inkster, as the Commissioner of the Royal Canadian Mounted Police, where he had spent his career. Controlling was obviously important, as was linking, to ensure no surprises for the politicians.[46] But above all, Norm functioned on the collective level of leading, to protect and strengthen the culture of the force, which was legendary.

Linking Outside, on the People Plane

Research has demonstrated that managers are external linkers as much as they are internal leaders. They build networks of outside contacts, partly to bring information into the organization, but also to lobby for its causes. Managers also represent their organization at ceremonial events, as figureheads.

> Carol Haslam brokered between partners and producers of the films, drawing on what seemed to be an immense web of contacts and a finely tuned understanding of British television. This was a particularly intricate process, involving a great deal of linking and juggling.
>
> At Ngara, Stephen Omollo met the representative of a major donor organization who came to audit the use of its money in the camps. Stephen's knowledge of the operations, illustrated in his detailed replies to many of the questions, was impressive—informed, articulate, and straightforward.

Doing Inside, on the Action Plane

Managers rarely *do* directly, in the sense that workers do by making products and delivering services. So why do we often hear comments like "Mary-Anne is a doer." What this means is that, on the action plane, managers help other people to get things done—in the spirit of the French expression *faire faire*, to make something get made. They champion changes, handle disturbances, join projects to influence their outcomes, and so on.

> Jacques Bentz, number two executive at GSI, a French high-tech firm, was an active participant in a meeting about a software platform being developed for the French post office. He gave advice and, at the end of the meeting, pushed for what was needed next. Asked why he attended, Jacques replied that the project was setting a precedent for the company, "the beginning of a strategy."

Dealing Outside, on the Action Plane

Dealing is the other side of doing, its external manifestation. Managers negotiate with unions, do deals with funders, work with partners in joint ventures.

> Fabienne Lavoie, as head nurse on the surgical ward, dealt with the doctors. John Cleghorn, as CEO of the Royal Bank of Canada, lunched with financial investors. Brian Adams, as Canadair program manager, negotiated all kinds of arrangements with partners.

Well-Rounded Managing

Putting all this together while looking back at Figure M6.1, we can conclude that managing has to be well-rounded. In other words, managers must give attention to all the roles. Can you imagine a manager who never issues an order, never does a deal, or never builds a network of contacts? Of course, a manager can tilt to one role or another, depending on the job and its immediate circumstances, as in the case of a factory foreman ever prepared to handle a disturbance, or an entrepreneur always ready to do a deal. But a manager who tilts too far, or for too long, can send the organization oscillating out of control, like a lopsided load in a washing machine. Hence, **effective managers exhibit a dynamic balance across all the roles, on all the planes, internally and externally**.

> Carol Haslam of the film company could afford to manage neither exclusively out nor exclusively in, although she had to use a different style for each. I described it as "hard dealing and soft leading." She used her vast array of contacts to "do the deals" of film contracts, and once done, she had to assemble a team, thereafter, not to control it so much as to monitor its progress.
>
> The remarkable thing in Fabienne's day on the nursing ward was how everything just seemed to blend together as she executed all the roles in a natural rhythm. A short conversation with a nurse combined controlling with sympathetic leading, followed by a linking call with a patient's relative, all this while she was constantly *doing* one thing and another. I described her work as blended care, quite a contrast with managing as interventionist cure.[47]

The world of managing might have been simpler when it was thought to be planning, organizing, coordinating, and controlling—simpler, but also simplistic.

Three Insights to deMYTHtify Managing as Controlling

We start by debunking the fashionable image of the manager as orchestra conductor. The reality is in the rehearsals, not the show. The next Insight considers the impact of the Internet on the characteristics of managing. And the third describes the conundrums of managing that render control so difficult.

The Characteristics of Conducting

Here are three quotes that I found from prominent observers of managing. As you read them, let's play a little game. Please vote for the quote that best explains your own understanding of managing. But there's a trick: you must vote as soon as you read each one, even before you have read the others. But there's a compensating trick: you can vote up to three times!

Our first quote is from Peter Drucker, the guru's guru: "One analogy [for the manager] is the conductor of a symphony orchestra, through whose effort, vision and leadership, individual instrumental parts that are so much noise by themselves, become the living whole of music. But the conductor has the composer's score: he is only an interpreter. The manager is both composer and conductor."[48]

Your vote for the manager as composer and conductor?

Our second quote is from Sune Carlson, a prominent economist who studied the managing directors of nine Swedish companies: "Before we made the study, I always thought of a chief executive as the conductor of an orchestra, standing aloof on his platform. Now I am in some respects inclined to see him as the puppet in the puppet show with hundreds of people pulling the strings and forcing him to act in one way or another."[49]

Your vote for the manager as puppet?

Our third quote is from Leonard Sayles, management professor at Columbia University, who studied the work of middle managers in the United States: "The manager is like a symphony orchestra conductor, endeavoring to maintain a melodious performance...while the orchestra members are having various personal difficulties, stage hands are moving music stands, alternating excessive heat and cold are creating audience and instrumental problems, and the sponsor of the concert is insisting on irrational changes in the program."[50]

Your vote for the manager as being interrupted?

I use this game when I do workshops with managers. The results are inevitably the same. Few vote for the first (likely because they are suspicious of what's coming next), and a few more vote for the second. But when I read the third, all the hands go up! Managers are like orchestra conductors all right, but away from the "show." Does this mean they have no control? No, it means that they have to nuance whatever control they do have.

Why, then, is there this obsession with the maestro myth?[51] It is so ingrained, so grand, that would-be leaders can actually sign up for leadership workshops orchestrated by conductors, presumably there to imagine themselves as managerial maestros on the podium: a flick of the baton, and purchasing opens; a wave of the wand, and marketing chimes in with manufacturing; a grand sweep of the arms, and HR, PR, and IT harmonize. It's a leader's dream—who needs management?

Except that it's all a show. During performance, the musicians sit in their pecking orders, every note predetermined. They barely look at the conductor—who, by the way, may be a guest conductor. Can you imagine a guest manager in an executive suite or on a shop floor?

Who is pulling the strings: Toscanini or Tchaikovsky? The musicians, in fact, but they are playing the notes written for their instrument by the composer, not the conductor. But with the composer long dead, and the audience so enthralled, it is the conductor who gets the acclaim, albeit with a wave or two to the musicians.

So, beware of metaphors that mesmerize, especially this one, the worst possible for management. Since all the world is not a stage, no manager belongs on the podium of lofty leadership.

The Impact of the Internet

I sketched out these ideas long ago, before the Internet descended upon us, and have revised them ever since, racing to stay ahead of the hype.[52]

Managing, as a practice, does not change fundamentally. The subject matter of managing certainly changes, all the time, as do the styles that some managers favor, but not the basic practice. There appears to have been one evident exception to this in recent times that should be having a significant effect on the characteristics of managing: digital technologies, including the Internet, and especially email, a medium of communication that has dramatically increased speed and volume. Has its impact on managing been likewise dramatic?

Judging by all the emails flying about, and the ubiquitousness of the mobile devices in managerial offices, it would certainly seem so. But the question is whether this has changed managing fundamentally. The answer appears to be yes and no.

No, because the Internet may be mostly reinforcing the very characteristics that have long been prevalent in managerial work, and yes, because this may be driving some of the practice of managing over the edge.

The Media and Their Messages

It is important to note, for starters, that compared with oral communication (as discussed earlier), this new medium remains thin. Like conventional mail, email is restricted by the poverty of words alone: there is no tone of voice to hear, no gestures to see, no presence to feel. (Do emojis or "LOL" really do it for you?) Hence, while these media may give the impression of putting managers "in touch," the only thing actually being touched is a keyboard. And this can exacerbate a long-standing problem in managing, namely allowing a fancy new technology to give the illusion of control.

On the telephone, people can interrupt, grunt, laugh out loud, argue; in meetings, they can nod in agreement or nod off in boredom. Effective managers pick up on such clues. With email, in contrast, you don't quite know how someone has reacted until the reply comes back, and even then, you can't be sure if the words were chosen carefully or sent in haste.

Marshall McLuhan wrote famously about the "global village" created by the new information technologies. But what kind of a village is this? In the traditional village, you chatted with your neighbor at the local market, the heart of community. In the global village, you click to trade shares on an electronic stock market, or to send a message to someone on the other side of the globe whom you may never have met. Much like those fantasy-ridden love affairs on the Internet, such relationships can remain untouched.

In organizations that function as communities, trust and respect are absolutely key. The Internet may facilitate networking, but networks are not communities; in fact, e-networking may be weakening communityship, in organizations and societies alike. While email extends the manager's contacts—everyone becomes within easy reach—this may come at the expense of deeper communication, say with colleagues down the hall. They are the ones who can become remote! (On MythSite.org /network, see "Networks Are Not Communities.")

The Effects of Email on Managing

One thing is certain: email increases the pace and pressures of managing, and likely the interruptions as well. A laptop on a desk is one thing, an iPhone in the pocket is quite another—the tether to the global village. With regard to the managers' orientation to action, the irony is that email, technically removed from the action, ups the action-orientation of managing: do it fast, reply NOW!

Managing over the Edge

The conclusion is that the Internet may not be changing the practice of management fundamentally so much as reinforcing its long-standing characteristics.[53] But the devil can be in this detail: **the Internet may be driving much management practice over the edge**, making it so frenetic that it becomes dysfunctional—too remote, too disconnected, too superficial. A senior governmental official I met boasted that he kept in touch with his staff by email early every morning. In touch with a keyboard perhaps, but with his staff?

The Inescapable Conundrums of Managing

Managing is replete with conundrums—difficulties that cannot be resolved, although, once recognized, they can be alleviated. Here are seven that reveal fuller implications of the characteristics and roles of managing.[54]

1. **The predicament of planning** This is the plague of every manager. How to get in deep when there is so much pressure to get it done? How to plan, strategize, just plain think, let alone think *ahead*, in such a hectic job?

2. **The quandary of connecting** Yesterday you were transplanting kidneys, today you are managing surgeons who are transplanting kidneys—about as different as two jobs can be. How to keep informed, when managing is, by its very nature, removed from the very thing being managed?

3. **The labyrinth of decomposition** The world of organizations is chopped into little pieces—departments and divisions, products and services, programs and budgets, silos and slabs. Managers, whose own work is fragmented, are supposed to oversee and integrate all these pieces. Where to find synthesis in a world so decomposed by analysis?

4. **The dilemma of delegating** Managers receive a great deal of informal information—opinion, hearsay, gossip. How is a manager to delegate when so much of their information is personal and oral?
5. **The ambiguity of acting** A manager who delays a decision to better understand the situation can hold everyone else back from acting. But a manager who leaps into action can drag everyone into a black hole. How to act decisively in a complicated, nuanced world?
6. **The riddle of change** Constant change can be as dysfunctional as a lack of change. How to manage change when there is the need to maintain continuity?
7. **The clutch of confidence** No one wants a manager who shrivels up, any more than one who always acts fearlessly. How to maintain a sufficient level of confidence without crossing over into arrogance?

How can any manager possibly deal with all these conundrums concurrently? By facing them. These conundrums are not distractions; they *are* managing. To manage is thus to get the balance right while walking on all these tightropes.

IV Three Myths About Analyzing

Myth 7	If you can't measure it, you can't manage it.
deMyth 7	Whoever measured management, let alone measurement?

Can we really quantify quality, calculate culture, even predict the potential for a truly novel product? (P&G initially believed the market for Pampers to be travel, not home.) In fact, has anyone ever succeeded in measuring management, let alone even bothered to measure measurement, beyond extolling its wonders? I guess, therefore, we shall have to cease managing management as well as measurement.

Let's try something real, right here. You are reading this book. You have a measure of how much it cost, also how much time you're spending to read it. So, please measure the benefits of doing this reading—what you are really learning (and I don't mean some subjective number on a ten-point scale). If you can't, should you stop reading this book—and every other book, for that matter—because you can't quantify its impact? Maybe, then, stop so much of living too, because most of the important things in life are hardly amenable to measurement—like love, respect, benevolence, chocolate.

Certainly, **in management, we must measure what we can, just so long as we don't pretend that we can measure everything that matters, moreover that measuring is all that matters.** So, let's burst this myth to save management from measurement.

We have to manage the unmeasurable no less than the measurable, maybe even more so, because we can get mesmerized by measurement. Measuring as a complement to managing is a fine idea: measure what we can, take seriously what we can't, and manage both. But measuring like mad is not a fine idea: it has destroyed its share of organizations—public, private, and plural. But before we get to that, let's consider the failings of measurement.

The Soft Underbelly of Hard Data

Numerical information is referred to as "hard data"—I'm not sure why—and is somehow considered superior to data that is "soft." Here is what an AI Overview on a Google search had to say about that (accessed November 5, 2025): "Hard data is *factual, objective,* and measurable information that can be *quantified* and *verified*... [also] *scientific.* Examples include GDP figures, sales numbers, and unemployment rates, which are distinct from 'soft data,' which is qualitative and based on *opinions* or *perceptions*"[55] (italics added).

As a friend of mine used to say, "Would you like this nice thin meat, or that thick crappy stuff?" In fact, the "nice thin" words above—*factual, objective, quantified, verified, scientific*—can be crappy. Yes, AI can be wrong. So, let's describe this soft underbelly of hard data.

Hard data tends to be late. Information takes time to "harden." Don't be fooled by the speed of those electrons racing around the Internet. Happenings first have to be recorded—this can take time—then sometimes aggregated into reports, which may have to await some schedule (like the end of the month). As a sales manager, which would you prefer: to hear a rumor that your major customer was seen playing golf with your competitor, or to read a report a month later indicating that you lost their business?

Hard data is inadequate. Alone, these data can be sterile, even impotent. "No matter what I told him," complained a subject of Kinsey's famous study of sexual behavior in the human male, "he just looked at me straight in the eye and asked 'How many times?' "[56] A little loss of nuance, no?

Hard data may describe, but does it explain? The report mentioned in the example above does not tell the sales manager why that customer was lost, but the rumor of playing golf can begin to do that. Likewise, a report might tell you how many people came to your food bank, but a few conversations with users might reveal important evidence about the quality of the food, the attitude of the staff, the culture of your organization. Likewise, consider that quintessential bottom line: the whole company wrapped up in one number. Think of all the life lost in that number.

A surprising amount of hard data is unreliable. They look good, all those definitive little numbers on a pretty little screen. But where did they come from? Lift up the rock covering that hard data and have a look at what's crawling underneath.

> The government are very keen on amassing statistics—they collect them, add them, raise them to the nth power, take the cube root, and prepare wonderful diagrams. But what you must never forget that every one of these figures comes in the first instance from the [village watchman] who just puts down what he pleases.[57]

And not only the watchman. In his account of "statistics and planning" in the British Air Ministry during World War II, Ely Devons wrote that the collection of such data was extremely difficult and subtle, demanding "a high degree of skill," yet it "was treated . . . as inferior, degrading and routine work on which the most inefficient clerical staff could best be employed."

Errors entered the data in all kinds of ways, even just treating months all the same despite the varying number of holidays. "Figures were often merely a useful way of summing up judgment and guesswork." Sometimes they were even developed through "statistical bargaining." "But, once a figure was put forward . . . no one was able by rational argument to demonstrate that it was wrong. And when those figures were called 'statistics,' they acquired the authority and sanctity of Holy Writ."

It is interesting how we can fool even ourselves with hard data. Consider this. If we bike up and down a mountain pass, we will do about four times as much uphill as downhill. How so, since we have done exactly the same distance each way? It's because we don't experience distance; we experience time. Distance is an abstraction in our brains—in this case, something to boast about—whereas time is what we feel in our body—something to sweat about. (I boast from experience!) Shouldn't that count for more than keeping score?

More hard data is arbitrary, biased, even distorted. Have you ever met a number that couldn't be gamed—say, a claim about quality ("99 44/100 percent pure"), a citation count for a professor (cite your own publications), also a performance report from a manager who wants a promotion?

In the early days of liver transplants, a surgeon in London operated on ten patients, two of whom died on the operating table.[58] Of the other eight, a previous cancer recurred in one, and she was not expected to recover. The new liver of another was failing—he would need a second transplant—and three of the remaining six patients were too sick to resume work. The surgeon was asked about his success rate: eight of ten, he reported, and it could be nine out of eleven after that second transplant. (He counted livers, not people.) An immunologist said seven out of ten; the managers of the hospital said six out of ten; and the nurses, who knew the patients best, said three out of ten. And the right answer is... Where to find the magic envelope to decide whether to continue this procedure?

All of this is not a plea for getting rid of hard data. That makes no more sense than getting rid of soft data. **This is a plea to cease being mesmerized by measurement.** We use hard facts to check out soft hunches, so why not use soft hunches to check out hard facts (for example, by eyeballing the numbers)?

What Are "Hard Data" Anyway?

Rocks are hard, but data? Electrons in a *hard drive* are hardly hard, while numbers on paper are called *soft copy*. *Hard* is the illusion of having turned something real into a number: Joe Blow is 2.7 on some psychologist's scale. That settles it for Joe.

Soft data, in contrast, looks to be fuzzy, ambiguous, subjective, based on opinions and perceptions, according to that AI search. Worst of all, it can be *intuitive*, sometimes no more than gossip, hearsay, impression. Such data can't even be transmitted electronically. Horror upon horror! Count them out.

There's an old joke that if you meet someone (from a country I won't mention), hit him in the face. He'll know why. Well, if you meet a number somewhere, challenge it. You'll learn why.

Measuring Like Mad in the Public, Private, and Plural Sectors

Measuring like mad has reached epidemic proportions. Managers can catch the disease by calling in consultants, attending a trade conference, reading a management magazine. Here we find another definitive best way, no matter which sector you are in—public sector government, private sector business, or plural sector community. (Two-sector politics, public vs private, is another myth that needs to be put to rest in favor of three-sector society—but that's in another book.[59]) Consider some examples:

Misuse of Measurement in Public Sector Government

A senior British civil servant was asked why his department was doing so much measuring. He replied: "What else can we do when we don't know what's going on?" How about getting on the ground to find out what's going on? And then using judgment to assess that? Remember *judgment*?

Government has no bottom line, but rather, multiple objectives, many of which cannot easily be quantified (diplomacy, defense, disaster relief). And how about public education, which has been so damaged by excessive measuring? I defy anyone to measure what a child really learns in a classroom. We need to engage students, not just examine them.

Misuse of Measurement in Plural Sector Health Care

Health care, too, has suffered from this obsession. Many community hospitals in the plural sector—namely not-for-profit—have likewise been driven to measure like mad by the governments or insurance companies that fund them, with dire consequences for their services.[60]

It may be easy enough to measure the efficiency of producing automobiles on an assembly line, but how about the efficiency of treating patients in a psychiatric ward? Even in an operating room? If you need a difficult operation, let me suggest that you find a surgeon with a high death rate. Not because they are incompetent, rather because they take on the difficult cases. (This example is not frivolous: there are stories of surgeons who refuse to take on such cases for fear of messing up their numbers.)

Accordingly, **beware of efficiency in government and health care, because it often reduces to economy, namely cutting measurable costs at the expense of difficult-to-measure benefits** (as discussed in an Insight below entitled "A Note on That Dirty Word *Efficiency*").

Overuse of Measurement in Private Sector Business

Much of business itself these days is likewise mismanaged in this worst way. Just because business has a measurable bottom line doesn't mean that it can escape the consequences of this epidemic. After all, it has other lines that don't lend themselves to easy measurement, such as sustainability and innovation, even decency. Firing workers in great numbers may help the bottom line, for a while, but what happens to the future of the enterprise and of a society made up of such enterprises? (See "Enough of MORE. We Need Better," on MythSite.org, about how stock markets are killing companies and communities.)

The *balanced scorecard* was created to deal with multiple objectives—to include culture, skills, and "human capital" (i.e., people), alongside profit. If only this scorecard were balanced. Its dice are loaded, because the costs and benefits of things economic are usually easier to measure than those that are social (as discussed in the Insight following, on efficiency).

Where Has All the Judgment Gone?

Remember judgment? It's still in my Oxford dictionary: "1. the critical faculty, discernment . . . 2. good sense." Judgment used to be a key to managing effectively, even if it was hidden in the dark recesses of the human brain (as discussed in Myth 9). And then along came measurement, in the dazzling light. It was a good idea, until it replaced judgment. So please sing along:

Where has all the judgment gone?
Long time pausing.
When has all that judgment gone?
Too long ago.
Where did all that judgment go?
Gone to numbers, one by one.
This leaves us on the brink.
When will we ever think?

(adapted by the author with apologies to Pete Seeger)

Some of My Favorite Quotes About Numbers

- Nothing spoils numbers faster than a lot of arithmetic. (*Peanuts*)
- I stood up to be counted and they told me to take a number.
- Quality has two enemies: quantity and equality. (Salvador de Madariaga)
- Yogi Berra, when asked if he would like his pizza cut into four or six pieces, said, "You'd better make it four. I don't think I can eat six pieces."

Two Insights to deMYTHtify Measurement

One describes how economists did a number on a precious idea. The other questions the motherhood word efficiency.

How National Happiness Became Gross[61]

The tiny kingdom of Bhutan, wedged between Tibet and India, became famous for coming up with Gross National Happiness (GNH), thanks to an enlightened king. GNH resonated with people around the world who were fed up with Gross National Product (GNP). It was based on four "pillars" (good governance, sustainable development, preservation and promotion of culture, and environmental conservation), elaborated in nine "domains" (including health, education, psychological well-being, and community vitality). Simple enough.

Curious about this GNH, I visited Bhutan in 2006. Two things struck me in discussions about this with a number of the country's knowledgeable people. First, they had no idea how to measure much of GNH. Second, this didn't much matter because the country seemed to behave true to its precepts. Measureless, they got the idea. As a BBC reporter put it, GNH had become "a way of life" in Bhutan—a poor country where life seemed to be rather pleasant.

Not long after this, economists descended on Bhutan to fix GNH, even though it wasn't broken. After all, if the Bhutanese didn't measure GNH, how could they possibly manage it? Soon each of the nine domains had "its own weighted and unweighted GNH index . . . analyzed using . . . seventy-two indicators. . . . Mathematical formulas have even been developed to reduce happiness to its tiniest component parts." One survey, which took five to six hours to complete, "included about 750 variables." These technocrats attended to the gross all right, but how about the happiness?

Critics of GNH have challenged its subjective judgments. Economics professor Deirdre McCloskey criticizes such measurements as unscientific, making the analogy that society could not "base physics on asking people whether today was 'hot, nice, or cold.' " If only education, culture, and happiness were as measurable as the temperature. I wonder if the greater threat to GNH has come from the friends who want to measure it or the enemies who want to eradicate it.

Not long after my visit, Tshering Tobgay, an ex-student of Michael Porter, the Harvard strategy guru, became prime minister. Soon he was claiming that GNH "distracted [some people] from the real business at hand," namely "the bottom line . . . that we have to work harder." This he could understand, in contrast to GNH, which he found "very difficult." In fact, he claimed that he found it to be "complicating stuff." Can happiness without measurement really be confusing stuff?

A Note on That Dirty Word *Efficiency*[62]

Efficiency gets us the greatest bang for the buck, to use an old military expression. Herbert Simon, winner of one of those non-Nobel prizes in economics, called efficiency a value-free, completely neutral concept. You decide what benefits you want; efficiency gets you them at the least possible cost. Who could argue with that? Me, for one.

I became suspicious when I wondered why *efficiency* had become a dirty word in so many places. (Consider the label "efficiency expert.") I concluded that the problem lies, not in the definition of the word, but in its application in practice.

I list below a couple of places as being efficient. Ask yourself to what aspect of the place this refers—don't dwell, just let the first word pop into your head.

A restaurant is efficient.

Did speed of service pop in? It does for most people, but rarely the quality of the food. Is that how you usually choose your restaurant? (Years ago, when I asked my father about this, he said, "If I heard that a restaurant was efficient, I would wonder about the food.")

My house is efficient.

Energy consumption always comes out way ahead. Tell me: how many people buy a house for its energy consumption, compared, say, with its location?

What's going on here? It's quite obvious, as soon as we realize it. **When we hear the word *efficiency*, we zero**

Some of My Favorite Quotes About Experts

- For every expert, there is an equal and opposite expert. (Arthur C. Clarke)
- An expert is someone with no elementary knowledge. (Mark Twain)
- An economist is someone who has never met a real person but once had one described to them.
- In science as in love, a concentration on technique is likely to lead to impotence. (Peter L. Berger)
- An actuary is someone who would have been an accountant, but couldn't stand the excitement.

in—subconsciously—on the most measurable criterion, like speed of service or consumption of energy. *Efficiency* means *measurable* efficiency, implicitly. The cult of efficiency thus reduces to the cult of calculation. As a consequence, efficiency is not neutral at all, since it favors what is most easily measured. And herein lies the problem, in three respects.

1. **Because costs are usually easier to measure than benefits, efficiency often reduces to economy: cutting measurable costs at the expense of less measurable benefits.** Think of all those governments that have cut the measurable costs of health care or education while the less measurable quality of those services has deteriorated. In business, some of the greatest disasters have been traced back to CEOs who cut budgets for quality control to up the bottom line right away.

2. **Because economic costs are typically easier to measure than social costs, efficiency can result in an escalation of social costs**—which economists treat as "externalities." Making a factory or a school more efficient is easy, so long as you don't care about the air or the minds that get polluted. That is how efficiency gets a bad name.
3. **Because economic benefits are typically easier to measure than social benefits, efficiency drives us toward an economic mindset that can result in social degradation.** More simply, we are efficient when we eat fast food instead of good food.

So, beware of efficiency, and of efficiency experts, as well as of efficient education, health care, even eating. Favor effectiveness. *Bon appetit!*

Myth 8 Proper strategies are planned.

deMyth 8 Interesting strategies are learned.

No one best way has infiltrated organizations as much as strategic planning. Nor has any incited more frustration. Every self-respecting organization—from local library to global conglomerate—must have a strategic plan, if only to get a loan from a bank or pretend to let board members know what's going on. Yet time and again, I have heard people complain bitterly about the process, asking why they must engage in what feels like a ritual. Strategic planning may well be the one worst way parading as the best.

What Is Strategic Planning Anyway?

Let me be clear. An organization can call anything it likes "strategic planning," for example, a retreat in the mountains to talk about the future. That's fine, but here I am referring to the formal technique, as promoted by so many books and consultants as the proper way to formulate strategy.

Here is how strategic planning is supposed to work, albeit a bit caricatured. Executives at the top work with planners to formulate strategy on schedule, to be implemented by everyone else. The process is articulated as a sequence of steps, each in its own box, beginning with industry analyses and ending with the programming of the result through operating plans (budgets, targets, and the like). Somewhere in between, strategy is supposed to get formulated, but about

FIGURE M8.1. **Roles of the Strategic Planner**

how, the charts remain silent, except for boxes like "Apprehend Inputs" and "Add Insights." (Seriously—I took this from the chart of an article on strategic planning.[63]) As Gary Hamel, a sage strategy guru, put it: "The dirty little secret is that we don't have a theory of strategy creation. We don't know how it's done."[64] The result of all this strategic planning is that organizations often end up, not with new strategies so much as with the extrapolation of the strategies they already have, perhaps with modifications in product and market positions. Or else, they simply copy the strategy of some competitor. (Have a look at the strategies of so many big banks and phone companies.)

More commonly, what is called *strategic planning* reduces to *strategic programming*: not to create new strategies but to operationalize the strategies that have been created by other means, by making operating plans that set targets and allocate budgets—in a supermarket chain, for example, specifying how many new stores to build, on what schedule, at what cost, and so on. Here, again, we find numbers galore, as if they alone add up to a fresh new strategy

This is what renders so much **strategic planning an oxymoron: it plans, not the strategy, but the consequences of strategy.** Figure M8.1 thus shows strategic planning as a black box, with planners taking their place outside of it: feeding their analyses in and programming the consequences out.

Many Pitfalls, One Grand Fallacy

What's the problem? Above all, it is the failure to get the message of Frederick Taylor's work. Strategic planning can be seen as the final step in his quest for scientific management, which began on the shop floor and ends in the executive suite. But while Taylor studied every process he wished to change in meticulous detail, formal strategic planning persists with no apparent appreciation of how strategies actually get made.

In my book, *The Rise and Fall of Strategic Planning*, I used the quote that "an expert is someone who avoids all the many pitfalls on their way to the grand fallacy."[65] This literature is replete with warnings about the pitfalls to be avoided in strategic planning, for example, losing the support of top management, or letting politics get in the way. **What gets missed in strategic planning is its grand fallacy: that you can't get synthesis from analysis**.

Analysis breaks things into their component parts, synthesis pulls them together. Analysis without synthesis reduces an organization to a skeleton of itself—a collection of bones with nothing holding them together, no sinew and muscle, no flesh and blood, no spirit and soul. It's not that organizations don't need analysis; it's that they need it as an input to synthesis.

When Michael Porter, strategy's best-known guru, claimed "I favor a set of analytical techniques for developing strategy," he was illustrating this grand fallacy: techniques don't develop strategy; *people* do, when they synthesize beyond analysis.[66] (In my more cynical moments, I define a technique as something you use instead of a brain.) What strategic planning does manage to synthesize, ironically, is our myths of managing: lofty leadership at the top, measuring like mad, remote control to centralize and formalize the bureaucratic form of organizing. Where's the place for experience and communityship?

To open this black box, to understand how strategies get made, we need to introduce three more definitions of strategy beyond plan: as pattern, position, and perspective.

Strategies as Realized Patterns, Aside from Intended Plans

In an exercise I have done with many groups of managers over the years, I begin by asking, "What's the first meaning that comes into your head when I say the word *strategy*?" Almost everyone says plan, direction, vision, or some other word about going forward. (Dictionaries, too, from my Oxford English: "a plan designed to achieve a particular long-term aim.")

Next, I ask them to think back to what the strategy of their organization was five years earlier, in other words, what strategy was intended then—perhaps as described in a strategic plan or report to the board. Then I ask them to consider the strategy the organization actually pursued over the ensuing five years—the strategy realized. And here comes the key question: Was the strategy that the organization realized over these five years the same as the strategy that it intended five years earlier? I give them three choices: (a) yes, mostly, (b) no, hardly, and (c) somewhere in between.

The result has been inevitably the same: a few people say yes and a few say no, but the vast majority always put themselves in between. What's going on? Well, for one thing, they should have refused to answer my question about the strategy actually

Plan

pursued, because it violates their own and the dictionary's definition of the word. Strategy is supposed to mean going forward, not looking backward. But they answer it willingly, because strategy is one of those words that we commonly define in one way, yet frequently—if not consciously—use in another. We do this because restricting use of the word *strategy* to "plans forward" is insufficient to understand strategic behavior. We also have to understand it as what the organization actually did.

In other words, **strategy may be defined by intention, but it is realized in action.** As shown in the little figures, **an intended strategy looks ahead, as some sort of plan into the future, while a realized strategy looks back, to some pattern, or consistency, in the actions taken by an organization, whether or not intended.**

In fact, we search for patterns in the behavior of organizations all the time, and when we find one—some convergence in what happened—we often label it a strategy. For example, a company that sees its competitor raising prices of its products might infer a strategy of going up market. Journalists can do much the same thing. For example, "The tentative deal [is an] example of how GM's strategy boils down to doing a little bit of everything until the market decides where it is going."[67]

Emergent Learning Beyond Deliberate Planning

Once we understand this distinction between strategies as intended and realized, we can ask the question that busts open the myth of strategic planning: must all strategies be deliberate, that is, **must a pattern realized in action necessarily follow from a plan intended in thought?** And the answer comes straight out of the results of this exercise I did with the managers: not necessarily, indeed, maybe not even commonly. (In the example from the journalist above, was GM thinking in this way, or maybe just acting in this way—responding to pressures in the marketplace?)

If we can act without deciding (as when getting tapped on a knee by a physician), then presumably an organization can create a strategy without having a plan, indeed, even in violation of the plan it has. Of course, this could be because the organization messed up. But it could also be because it learned on the way to a new, realized, strategy, maybe because the world had the nerve to change in a way that was inconsistent with the plan.

As shown in Figure M8.2, intended strategies that are realized can be labeled *deliberate*, while some others can remain *unrealized*. But most interesting are those patterns that are realized without being intended; in other words, the organization learned as it

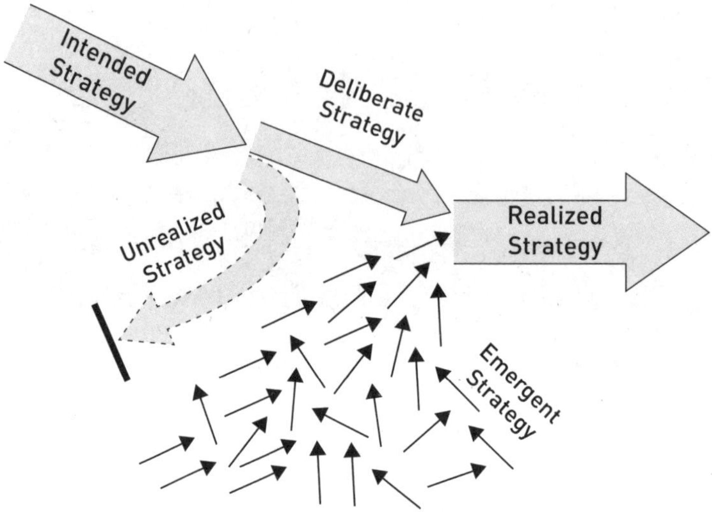

FIGURE M8.2. Forms of Strategy

went along, action by action, which eventually converged into a pattern. We can call this an ***emergent* strategy**.

Can this be common? Sure, when an organization is in a learning mindset more than an analytic one. Strategy making walks on two feet—one deliberate, the other emergent. Just as purely deliberate strategy precludes learning, so purely emergent strategy precludes control. The most successful strategies seem to fall in between.

Interestingly enough, emergent strategy can reverse the sequence of formulation to implementation. **An organization that becomes aware of a successful pattern that has emerged can formalize that into a deliberate strategy going forward.** To quote Søren Kierkegaard, "Life can only be understood backwards, but it must be lived forwards."

Position

Strategies as Tangible Positions and Broad Perspective

We still need two more definitions to fully understand the processes by which strategies are created. While the first two definitions looked forward and back, at process, these two—*position* and *perspective*—look up and down, at content, as shown in the little figures.

Consider this question. When McDonald's introduced Egg McMuffin, to bring people into its restaurants for breakfast, was this a strategic change for the company? I have asked this of many groups of managers, and they always split: some say, yes, of course, it was a new product in a new market, while others say, oh, come on, it's the same old thing, just with new ingredients.

Perspective

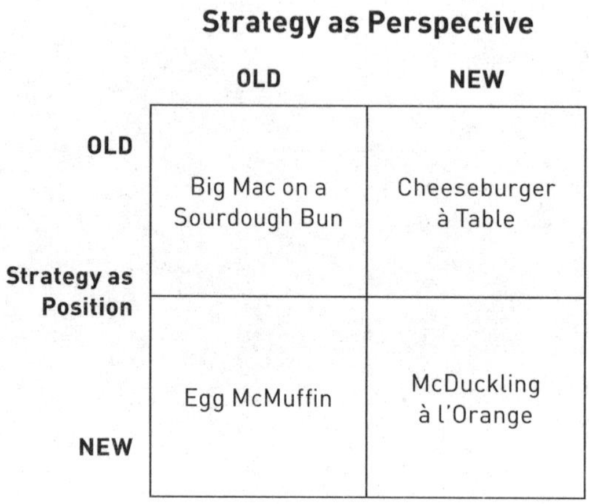

FIGURE M8.3. The Egg McMuffin Syndrome

Both are right: they just differ in how they define the content of strategy. The first sees strategy as tangible positions—products in markets—which Michael Porter has favored in his writing on Competitive Strategy,[68] while the other sees strategy as broad perspective, much as Peter Drucker wrote about "the theory of the business."[69] As illustrated in the little figures, position looks down, to the X that marks the spot—where the product meets the user—while perspective looks up, to an overall vision of the enterprise, its worldview.

The matrix in Figure M8.3 plots four possibilities with regard to old and new position and perspective. Egg McMuffin is in the lower left corner—a new position within McDonald's existing perspective. McDuckling à l'Orange, the opposite, shown on the lower right—would be a new position in a new perspective. But don't book a table quite yet: few organizations stray that far from their existing strategy. But what they sometimes do, shown on the upper right, is to change perspective in order to retain an existing position. An airline facing a discount competitor may have to alter its fundamental way of doing business just to keep its current customers. Of course, in the upper left is what most organizations do most of the time, namely, not mess with strategic positions or perspective at all—for example, by offering a Big Mac on a sourdough bun.

The Strategy Process as Planning, Learning, Visioning, and Venturing

OK, so now, with these four Ps for strategy—plan and pattern, position and perspective—we can open up that black box, to delineate four modes to create strategy, shown in yet another two-by-two matrix, in Figure M8.4—labeled planning, learning, visioning, and venturing. As we shall discuss, they map rather well on to the four forms of organizations discussed in Myth 3.

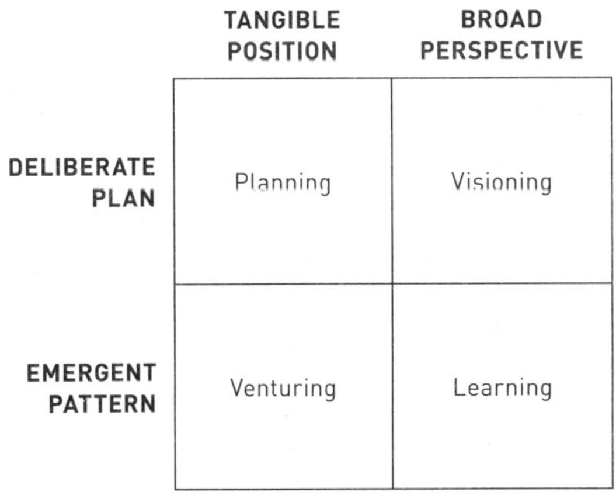

FIGURE M8.4. Four Strategy Modes

The Planning Mode

This mode was described earlier, with deliberate strategies formulated by senior managers, and staff planners using analytical techniques, to be implemented by everyone else in the organization. **Whatever new strategies come out of the planning process are more likely to augment the organization's portfolio of existing strategic positions than to create a new strategic perspective. Or else, strategic planning gets reduced to the strategic programming of the strategies the organization already has.**

Strategic planning tends to be favored in the programmed machine form of organization, with its propensity to control most everything. Put differently, strategic planning fine-tunes the programmed organization: the numbers do the planning.

We have done extensive research that tracks the strategies of organizations, from a supermarket chain to a university (ten of these studies are reported in my book *Tracking Strategies*).[70] They offer some good examples of these modes of strategy making.

> Because of the routine nature of their operations, also the need for stability and security, airlines are the quintessentially programmed machines, hence, they plan extensively and carefully. We tracked the strategies of Air Canada across forty years of its early history, during which the organization, set on a clear strategic course, remained there. We titled this study "Does planning impede strategic thinking?"

The Learning Mode

This mode falls at the other extreme: it is emergent, about learning the way to a new strategic perspective. Instead of assuming, as did Frederick Taylor, that workers have hands but not heads, **the learning mode assumes that a new strategy can form wherever people have the opportunity to learn strategically from their grounded experience.** We hear a good deal about Kaizen, the process in Japan whereby workers make suggestions for continuous improvements. Here we can consider *strategic Kaizen*: suggestions from the base that can change the strategy of the whole organization.

The IKEA concept of the flatpack—selling its furniture unassembled, for the cost and convenience of the company as well as its customers—provides a wonderful example.[71] This strategy, that changed not only the company, but the industry, did not come from any central planning process, not even from some executive committee. A designer had to deliver a table for a photo shoot, but he couldn't fit it in his car. So he thought to himself, *Why not take off the legs?* Then came the strategic moment: if we have to take the legs off, why not do so for the customers?

The project organization is especially suited to this mode of strategic learning, since each project has the potential to be a learning process unto itself, possibly taking the organization in a new strategic direction.

> The National Film Board of Canada (NFB), a quintessential adhocracy, with each film a project in its own right, became renowned for its short documentary films. We tracked almost three thousand of its films over almost four decades, to discern patterns as strategies. One offered the ultimate example of emergent strategy. At one point, the NFB suddenly branched into longer feature films, a new strategic position, with a different

strategic perspective. Where did this come from? Not from any planning process of senior management. In fact, it came as a surprise to both management and the filmmakers themselves. A film ran too long, and not being able to distribute it in the NFB's usual ways, it was marketed as a feature film in theaters. Other filmmakers took notice—*Why not me?*—and before long, some were making feature films of their own, thus taking the organization to a new strategic position and perspective—formulated by no one.[72]

The Visioning Mode

This mode falls between planning and learning, in the sense that it is centralized around the senior management, as in the planning mode, but is not systematically analytical so much as personally intuitive—strategy as a form of art. Here, a single visionary, usually the chief—personally in close touch with both organization and industry—learns his or her way to a new strategic perspective.

Once established, this perspective is deliberate, but **the visionary perspective serves as a deliberate umbrella under which specific strategic positions can emerge**, through the efforts of other people. Hence, a visionary strategy can be described as deliberately emergent. Above all, the vision must be kept informal and personal to allow it to remain robust, responsive, and inspirational. As Warren Bennis has written, you can tell a vision because "the first time you hear it, you'll never forget it." (Compare this with the following comment by an executive in a different place: "Sometimes I feel like a rhinoceros who doesn't see well and whose power of concentration is terrible; he charges at something that's a long way off, then forgets where he's going and stops to eat grass." No vision here!) Evidently, the visioning mode fits most naturally in the personal form of organization, where so much revolves around the chief.

> Sam Steinberg was an example of this in our research.[73] He took his company from a single grocery store to a chain of supermarkets that dominated the Montreal market. During the sixty years that we tracked its strategies, we saw only two changes in strategic perspective: a shift to self-service in the 1930s, which started in one of their eight stores overnight, and its movement into the shopping center business in the 1950s. With the arrival of the first one in Montreal, Sam Steinberg realized that he had to own them to ensure that his stores were in them.

The Venturing Mode

This mode also sits between planning and learning, but differently so. Here, as in the expression of "letting a thousand flowers bloom," **all kinds of people anywhere in the organization can champion their own strategic initiatives, which together add up to a portfolio of strategic positions.** These initiatives may or may not be deliberate for their champions, but they tend to be emergent for the organization that doesn't plan them.

> From our tracking strategy research, our study of McGill University across 150 years of its history provides a good example. Overall, in terms of strategic perspective, McGill remained rather undistinguished, even though its international reputation has long been distinguished. Like other research-oriented

universities, it has offered education and conducted research in pretty much every university domain—arts and science, engineering, management, medicine, and so on—distinguished mainly by where it does so: in Montreal.

Looking closer, however, one sees something quite different: McGill, again, like other such universities, has all kinds of unique strategic positions, such as the management development programs discussed in Myth 5. Such innovation does not usually come from any central vision or planning. Rather, these programs are ventures championed by the professors themselves, whether alone or in small teams, within their own field. In other words, lurking beneath the surface of many a standard-looking university can be found all kinds of interesting strategic positions. They practice distributive management, with a vengeance.

Some strategic venturing can, of course, be found in most organizations: they innovate, somewhere, somehow. What distinguishes universities, however, likewise general hospitals and other professional organizations, is that their portfolio of strategic positions *is* their strategy.

Can the sum of a bunch of rather autonomous ventures really be said to add up to a strategy for an organization? Yes, indeed, because together these ventures define how it positions itself in its world.

Thus, we have four quite different modes by which strategies can be created. Our world of organizations may have been simpler when strategic planning was thought to do it all. Simpler, but simplistic.

Three Insights to deMYTHtify Strategic Planning

The first two Insights are metaphors that contrast deliberate with emergent strategy—a hothouse model and a grassroots model.[74] *The third is a plea to stop blaming implementation when a strategy fails.*

A Hothouse Model of Strategy Formulation

Searching for a strategy? Here's how to get one, according to just about everything written on the subject, stylized here only slightly.

1. The senior management is the planter of all strategy. Consultants can offer advice (sometimes even the strategy itself—but don't tell anybody).
2. These strategies are intended to grow like tomatoes that are cultivated in a hothouse. The planners fertilize this growth with numbers galore.
3. The strategy comes out of this process immaculately conceived and formally explicit, like ripe tomatoes that are ready for the market.
4. Here the ripe tomato strategies are sent to everyone else in the organization, for implementation. In other words, everyone but the strategists get their hands dirty, trying to make the strategies happen. When this fails, they get blamed.
5. Hence, to manage the strategy process is to do the proper analyses, preconceive insightful strategies, and plant them carefully, then expect other people to grow them on schedule.

Wait, don't go off and start formulating your strategy quite yet. Read the next model first.

A Grassroots Model of Strategy Formation

How about this instead?

1. Strategies grow initially like weeds in a garden; they are not cultivated like tomatoes in a hothouse. They can *form*, rather than having to be *formulated*, meaning that they can spring up unexpectedly. The hothouse, if needed, can come later.
2. These strategies can take root in all kinds of places, wherever people have the capacity to learn and the resources to support that capacity. The point is that organizations cannot always plan where a strategy will appear. So, the best bet is to prepare fertile ground, where ideas can take root and grow vigorously.
3. Individual ideas become organizational strategies when they spread through the organization, much as weeds can proliferate to encompass a whole garden. After all, what's a weed but a plant that wasn't expected? With a change of perspective, the emerging strategy can become what's valued. Bear in mind that Europeans enjoy salads of the leaves of dandelions, America's most notorious weed.
4. There is a time to sow strategies and a time to reap them. Blurring the distinction between sowing and reaping can damage a garden—and an organization too. Managers have to appreciate when to exploit an established crop of strategies, and when to encourage new strains to replace them.
5. Hence, to manage this process is not to preconceive deliberate strategies, but to create a climate—a culture—within which a wide variety of strategies can take root. While a truly destructive weed, once noticed, is best uprooted immediately, one that seems capable of

bearing fruit is worth watching, in fact, sometimes worth ignoring until the plant withers, or else fruit appears, at which point a hothouse can be built around it.

Stop Blaming Implementation

Strategic planning assumes a fundamental separation between formulation and implementation: the head thinks so that the hands can act. But what happens when a strategy fails? What gets blamed, formulation or implementation?

Implementation, inevitably, perhaps because the formulators do the blaming: "You dumbbells weren't smart enough to implement our brilliant strategy." If these dumbbells were smart, they would reply: "If you're so smart, why didn't you formulate a strategy that we dumbbells, whom you are supposed to know all too well, were capable of implementing?"

Hence, **every failure of implementation can be described as a failure of formulation**: what's the use of a strategy that can't be implemented by the people who are supposed to do that? But what we really need to question is the **assumption that the formulator is sufficiently informed, and the situation is sufficiently stable, or predictable, to ensure that no reformulation will be necessary during implementation.** Trouble is, these days, the unexpected is perhaps more likely to be expected than ever, but, as always, we don't know how to predict discontinuities.

Some of My Favorite Quotes About Predicting the Unpredictable

- A long-range weather forecast should be obtained before leaving, as weather conditions are extremely unpredictable. (*Natal Daily News, June 16, 1982*)
- Comment from a researcher in British Foreign Office from 1903 to 1950: Year after year the worriers and fretters would come to me with awful predictions of the outbreak of war. I denied it each time. I was only wrong twice.
- I think there is a world market for maybe five computers. (Thomas J. Watson, President of IBM, 1948)
- Atomic energy might be as good as our present-day explosives, but it is unlikely to produce anything very much more dangerous. (Winston Churchill, 1939)
- Not within a thousand years will man ever fly. (Wilbur Wright, 1901)

And here's an anecdote in response to the last three:

Two guys hiking in the Rockies encounter a grizzly bear. One takes off like a shot. The other calls to him: "Why are you running, you know you can't outrun a grizzly bear." He calls back: "I don't have to outrun the grizzly bear. I only have to outrun you!"

Watson had to outrun his competitors; Churchill, the Russians; Wright, himself.

Myth 9 To make decisions, think in order to act.

deMyth 9 How about acting in order to think, also seeing in order to act?

Let's start with probably the most important decision of your life: choosing a mate. Having been conditioned to think before you act, you make a list of the criteria you are looking for in a partner, say, if female, brilliant, beautiful, and bashful. Then you list all the possible candidates. Next comes the analysis: you score each candidate on each of the criteria. Finally, you add up all the scores to find out who won and inform the lucky lady—only to hear her say this: "While you were going through this rigmarole, I got married, and now I have a little baby." *Thinking first* can have its little disadvantages.

If you are like most people, however, you proceeded differently. One day, you turned a corner, and there s/he was. Done! It's called love at first sight, although here I prefer to call it *seeing first*: you see in order to act.

These days, however, many choose a third way. They *act first,* in order to *think after*: meet someone who might be right, live together for a while to find out, and then decide—or maybe they *don't* decide—they just stay together...

Thinking First

Read almost everything that's been written about decision making, and you have to conclude that thinking first is not only the best way, but the only way: we must diagnose, then design (to find or create alternative solutions), then decide, and finally do—in that order.

In some circumstances, this works fine. Arranged marriages in India, when the parents think first, apparently have a lower divorce rate than love marriages. But, as noted, thinking first can have its disadvantages too. We can be too cerebral, too calculating—in both senses of the word. **The message here is not to suspend thinking, but to put it in its place, alongside seeing and doing.**

Years ago, we studied twenty-five decision processes in organizations, by delineating in detail all the steps that were taken in each.[75] These processes turned out to be a lot more convoluted than you might think. In a decision about building a new plant, for example, the process kept cycling back—interrupted by unexpected events, diverted by new opportunities—going round and round until finally a solution emerged. This ending may have been as clear as a wave breaking on the shore, but explaining how it came to be was more like trying to trace the origin of that wave back into the ocean. Sometimes, however, we are mystified by the final choice: it just seems to erupt, out of nowhere. Here is how Alexander Kotov, the chess grandmaster, described a sudden insight that followed a lengthy analysis:

> So, I mustn't move the knight. Try the rook move again.... At this point you glance at the clock. My goodness! Already thirty minutes gone on thinking about whether to move the rook or the knight. If it goes on like this, you'll really be in time trouble. And then suddenly you are struck by the happy idea—why move rook or knight? What about B-QN 1? And

without any more ado, without analysis at all, you move the bishop. Just like that.[76]

Seeing First

One day, my father announced to my grandmother, "Today I met the woman I'm going to marry!" And that he did. There was not a lot of analysis in this decision, I assure you, but it worked out well. Even some rather formal decisions happen this way, by seeing in order to do—for example, deciding to hire someone seconds into an interview. Such decisions are not necessarily whims; they can be *insight*ful.

Insight—seeing into—suggests that decisions may be driven as much by what is seen as by what is thought. In W. Köhler's well-known 1920s experiment, a chimpanzee struggled to reach a banana placed high in its cage.[77] Then it *saw* a box in the corner, made the connection, moved the box under the banana, climbed aboard, and its problem was solved. The same can be true for strategic vision, which can depend on seeing an opportunity that others miss. The world is so rich and varied that if you see it as it really is, rather than as you thought, you could become a better strategist.

We are so conditioned to think; why are we not likewise conditioned to see? As a masters student at MIT, I had a professor of operations management, a sharp, practical guy, who did just that. One day, he asked one of us in class how many columns there were in the entrance hall to our building, a place we all walked through many times every day. The student didn't know, so the professor suggested he go have a look. When he came

Some of My Favorite Quotes About Thinking, Seeing, Doing

THINKING

- If everyone is thinking alike, then no one is thinking" (attributed to Benjamin Franklin and others)
- It requires a very unusual mind to undertake an analysis of the obvious. (Alfred North Whitehead)

SEEING

- The soul... never thinks without a picture. (Aristotle)
- [T]he structure was too pretty not to be true. (James Watson, in *The Double Helix*)
- You can observe a lot just by watching. (Yogi Berra)

DOING

- Ever tried? Ever failed? No matter. Try again. Fail again. Fail better. (Samuel Beckett)
- We will either find a way or make one. (Hannibal)
- They planned their campaigns, just as you might make a splendid piece of harness. It looks very well, and answers very well; until it gets broken; and then you are done for. Now I made my campaigns of ropes. If anything went wrong, I tied a knot, and went on. (Duke of Wellington)
- We are much more likely to act our way into a new way of thinking than to think our way into a new way of acting. (Karl Weick)

back, the professor looked him in the eye, and asked, "What color is the floor?" The next time the student came back, he could tell us everything about that hall!

Doing First

What happens when we can neither think nor see our way to a decision? We can *do* first: **try something and see how it works, in other words, act in order to think.** If it works well, we do more of it, if it doesn't, we try something else, until we find what does work well. It's called trial and error. Start small to learn big. Karl Weick, a professor of organization behavior, labeled this *sensemaking*: making sense of what works.[78]

Of course, doing first has its disadvantages too. Terry Connolly, a professor who studied decision making, explained this well: "Nuclear wars and childbearing decisions are poor settings for a strategy of 'try a little one and see how it goes.'"[79] But there are many other decisions for which this works. The electronics firms in Japan built up their businesses by flooding local test markets with all kinds of products, to see what sold, and then took those global.

Analysis and Intuition

Let's pick up here on the discussion in Myth 7 about analysis. Thinking first is rational, logical, preferably analytical. The word we tend to use for the alternative is *intuition*, which has a less positive connotation. Peter Drucker, the guru of management gurus, claimed in 1954 that "the days of the 'intuitive' manager are numbered."[80] We are still counting.

I define *intuition* as somehow knowing for sure, just not knowing why—why we know, and why for sure. By this definition, a hunch is not an intuition. Wayne Gretzky, the hockey superstar, captured this sense of intuition with his famous comment: "I skate to where the puck is going to be." Not maybe! No time to think first with the speed of that puck, he just had to act, based on his ingrained experience.

Yet that Drucker bias lives on. As we have seen throughout this book, **thinking first, especially in the form of analysis, remains a domineering best way—plan strategically, measure madly, organize hierarchically, control deterministically.**

The Great Divide, in Our Brains and Our Organizations

Analysis and intuition sit on either side of a great divide that plagues many of our organizations today. Managers on the ground battle with technocrats on upper floors who want to program everything. Some fascinating research has suggested that this divide comes straight out of our own heads, in our brains split into two hemispheres.

Here's the story. To relieve a patient's severe epileptic fits, which intensified as they crossed back and forth between the two hemispheres of his brain, physicians took the radical step of cutting the corpus callosum, the tissue that connects the hemispheres.

The seizures stopped, and he seemed normal, until a series of tests revealed that, being separated, the two hemispheres exhibited minds of their own, so to speak. As Robert Ornstein explained in a book entitled *The Psychology of Consciousness,* the right hemisphere (in right-handed people) is associated with spatial perception, dreaming, emotion, also of the "communication of gestures, facial and body movements, tone of voice."[81] In contrast, the left hemisphere is associated with language and logic. More broadly, the left hemisphere appears to be the seat of a mode of thinking that is linear, sequential, orderly, while the right hemisphere appears to be the center of a mode of thinking that is simultaneous, holistic, relational—one apparently analytical, the other more oriented to synthesis, a dichotomy we have been seeing throughout this book.

In 1976, I brought this finding into an article in the *Harvard Business Review* entitled "Planning on the Left Side and Managing on the Right," in reference to the sides of our bodies that respond to the opposite hemisphere of our brain.[82] I had just published my first book, *The Nature of Managerial Work,* and this research seemed to explain the difference I found between managing as formally depicted and managing as actually practiced—informal, intuitive, experienced-based.

Two Ways of Knowing

This suggests an important conclusion that I have been touching on throughout the book. Could it be that we have two ways of knowing, presumably one for each side of our brain? Some things we know formally, explicitly. We can verbalize them, perhaps because we've been exposed to them often—for example, that if we can't measure it, we can't manage it. Then there are those things that we know in our gut, informally, tacitly, based on our personal experience—for example, that we willingly manage all kinds of things that we have no clue how to measure.

Presumably, **we feel better when these two ways of knowing—formally and tacitly—correspond instead of contradict.** This may be why managers tell me they feel so good when they read my description of managerial work: this is how they experience it, with all its interruptions, etc., rather than as controlling, controlling, controlling, and controlling. In contrast is the feeling when, for example, consultants keep pushing a strategic planning process that just doesn't feel right. We might conclude that every organization needs a functioning corpus callosum that connects its great divide.

Two Insights to deMYTHtify Having to Think First

The first Insight suggests that design doing *may be a better concept than* design thinking. *The second calls for the recognition of serendipity in decision making.*

Design Doing

In a book entitled *The Sciences of the Artificial*, Herbert Simon wrote "Everyone designs who devises courses of action aimed at changing existing situations into preferred ones."[83] This includes not only architects who design buildings and engineers who design machines, but also managers who design decisions. As noted in the discussion above, designing happens between diagnosing and deciding. But how do we design? Maybe not as you might think.[84]

Four Approaches to Design

Jeanne Liedtka and I published an article entitled "Time for Design," in which we identified four approaches to designing.[85]

- A *formulaic* approach based on following preexisting principles more than engaging in open-ended experimentation
- A *visionary* approach that relies on the personal imagination of the designer, which can be more responsive to opportunity
- A *conversational* approach that opens the process beyond the designer, to the insights of the people who have to live with the design
- An *evolving* approach that enables the design process to keep adapting as situations change, problems arise, and opportunities appear

Apparently bees are inclined to follow a more formulaic approach, while flies tend to prefer an evolving one. Place half a dozen bees and the same number of flies in a bottle and lay it horizontally, with the closed end to the window, and you will find that the bees, in search of light but ignorant of glass, persist in trying to get through the glass at the base, whereas the flies, ignorant of both, going every which way, eventually find the opening and so free themselves. "It is [the bees'] love of flight, it is their very intelligence, that is their undoing.... [To them], glass is a supernatural mystery... whereas the feather-brained flies, careless of logic... flutter wildly hither and thither and... necessarily end up by discovering the friendly opening that restores their liberty to them."[86]

The moral of this story is that we need more flies making decisions and fewer bees.

Paving the Pathways

There is a park in Prague, likewise perhaps where you live, that was designed formulaically—by designers who knew better. They paved the pathways where they decided that the people of Prague should walk. One of these, designed to take people from a busy street to a bridge, was paved in an S-shape. So, the people of Prague, who really did know better about their own travel, took control of the situation and walked straight across, on the grass that became bare earth. Thus evolved the people's pathway to the Prague bridge. "Experts" who know better can be a menace to good design when they preclude the experience of the users, who may know more about their own needs.

Designing Doing

Design thinking has become a fashionable phrase. On its website, under "What Is Design Thinking?" the renowned design consultancy IDEO described it as an "iterative process" that proceeds through these phases: empathizing with the users, defining their needs, problems, and own insights, ideating by challenging assumptions and creating ideas for innovative solutions, prototyping to start creating solutions, and testing them.[87] They call this design *thinking*, but it reads more like *design doing*. Why not call it that?

Is Serendipity Serendipitous?[88]

If a cartoon character in *Peanuts* can claim that nothing spoils numbers faster than a lot of arithmetic, I guess there are people who think that nothing spoils decision making faster than a little serendipity. Let's entertain the opposite position.

Serendipity connects dots, unexpectedly and fortuitously—as in the famous examples of Post-it notes and penicillin pills. The former, from the company 3M, made use of a glue that was thought too weak to be useful, and the latter resulted from recognizing the potential of a mold that had killed bacteria in a sample in Alexandre Fleming's research laboratory.

But is serendipity truly serendipitous? In other words, do the dots connect themselves, through luck, by chance? Or is there more to it? I believe there is more to it. In fact, we should expect serendipity, and thus manage it.

Expecting Serendipity

Yuki and Yumi bump into each other on a street in Yonkers. They knew each other in Yokohama, but here, halfway around the world, they fell in love with each other at first sight. What an unexpected, fortuitous coincidence!

Had Yuki walked down a different street, or had Yumi left her hotel five minutes later, both might have remained single. Or else, back home, each might have met another serendipitous love, with a different story to tell. Put differently, **while the odds of one particular serendipitous event happening are low, the odds of any one of all the possible serendipitous events happening is not. Serendipity is more likely than we imagine.**

Everyday Serendipity

These thoughts came together (serendipitously?) when I was invited to make comments at a panel discussion about serendipity at the annual conference of the Academy of Management. There, one day before the panel, I had a meeting with my publisher, about a new book of mine. We discussed the possibility of creating an instructor's guide to help professors adopt it as a textbook, but we weren't sure how to proceed, other than wondering who might author it.

That evening, when I took the elevator to my room on the twenty-fifth floor, in came a woman who hit the button for the twenty-fourth floor. She said, "I really like your new book." To which, I replied, "You read it already?" and she explained that they were adopting it as a textbook.

So here came my "elevator pitch." During the floors we had left, I suggested that she might want to help us with the instructor's manual. When she responded positively, I managed to dig out a card with my email address before we arrived at her floor. Serendipitously, we were on the twenty-fourth and twenty-fifth floors instead of the fourth and fifth floors.

True, this was not an earth-shattering event, nothing like penicillin. But it was serendipitous nonetheless, at least potentially so. In fact, I counted about five other events that happened to me serendipitously at the same conference—chance encounters that could have led to something interesting. You see, serendipity is rather common, especially at conferences like this one. With more than ten thousand attendees, the possibilities were endless.

Indeed, isn't this a main reason why we go to such conferences? They are serendipity conferences—places to expect fortuitous chance encounters. Better to walk the halls than attend the presentations. Otherwise, you might return home disappointed, reporting to colleagues "Such a lousy conference, great talks but no serendipity." (At the same conference in a later year, I met my publishing buddy again. This time, he suggested I write a book like the one you are reading. Serendipitously, I had been thinking the same thing. So you, too, share in this bit of serendipity.)

Managing Serendipity

Serendipity can thus be managed. Wherever a manager experiences a chance encounter, serendipity can rear its playful head. Managers should, therefore, not only expect unexpected encounters, but also predispose themselves to finding them, and exploiting them, even if just by having a business card handy when taking an elevator.

Let me make a simple suggestion that goes along with this: **cherish anomalies**, occurrences that don't seem to fit with anything else, for instance, say one customer uses your product in a quirky way. Researchers, and other people too, tend to dismiss anomalies as inconvenient. Get on with the central tendencies; ignore the outliers. But what could be more serendipitous than an anomaly that can turn out to realign our beliefs?

Companies like 3M might be seen as serendipitous enterprises, organized to exploit unexpected discoveries, like the Post-it notes. They encourage their people to be mindful at all times, and that has to include anomalies. Likewise, many entrepreneurs can be seen as serendipitous panthers, ready to spring at the first sign of a potential opportunity. Such people are, after all, masters at connecting the dots.

For the sake of serendipity, therefore, let me suggest that you vacate office and home, to get into the thick of things, where the unexpected is more likely to happen. In this respect, please understand that COVID has done a number on serendipity, because it has driven so many people to work, isolated, at home. Serendipity happens when people bump into each other at the coffee machine. Did you ever bump into someone at a coffee machine after a Zoom call?

V The Mother of All Myths

Myth 10 **Our theory is true.**

deMyth 10 **No theory is true, but some are sometimes useful.**

A "fact" may or may not be true, and reality is certainly true, but no theory can ever be true. That's because it is not reality, but some simplification of reality. While a fact pertains to something specific—for example, that this book presents ten myths—a theory generalizes beyond the facts, to describe reality—for example, that managers plan, organize, coordinate, and control. The problem is that reality is vast and complicated, whereas theory is focused and limited—ultimately, just a bunch of words and symbols. No theory can ever be big enough to capture all of the reality in question.

Here is a prominent example. In 1492, Christopher Columbus discovered truth: that the Earth is round, not flat. Did he? Is it? When I look out my window, I see a lake, which looks flat, surrounded by hills, which look bumpy. Of course, seen from space, the Earth does look round, but that's because we can't discern its tiny little bumps, like Mount Everest. In actual fact, the Earth is not quite round: it bulges at the equator, making it slightly spheroid rather than perfectly spherical. This gives us yet another limited theory about the reality that is the Earth.

Were the Earth flat, Columbus would have sailed over the edge, and we would never have heard from him again. Lucky for him, it was rather round, at least on the seas that he sailed. And lucky for me, our lake is rather flat because when the ice forms I love to skate on it—and skating uphill can be tricky.

So, what are we to make of this? That I am going off theorizing about theory? No, this is important because, **while we must never take any theory to be true, we can often take some theories to be useful, but only under particular circumstances.**

The round earth theory worked fine for Columbus, sailing on the sea, just as the flat earth theory works fine for me, skating on the on the lake. (Imagine if I had to correct for the curvature of the lake every time I went skating.) You see, we make constructive use of all kinds of flawed theories. Donald Hebb, McGill's renowned psychologist, explained this rather nicely: "A good theory is one that holds together long enough to get you to a better theory."

Theory as Dogma

Many proper scientists don't get this. They battle with each other over their respective one best theory, without recognizing that each may be better and worse, depending on the circumstances. Einstein's theory of relativity debunked Newton's theory of mechanics. So what? We still make great use of the latter.

Some of My Favorite Quotes About Truth

- There are no whole truths; all truths are half-truths. (A.N. Whitehead)
- Add a few drops of malice to a half-truth and you have an absolute truth. (Eric Hoffer)
- Believe those who are seeking the truth. Doubt those who find it. (Andre Gide)
- Men occasionally stumble over the truth, but most of them pick themselves up and hurry off as if nothing happened. (attributed to Winston Churchill)
- All astrologers are liars. Even when an astrologer tells the truth, they are lying. (proverb)
- Seek simplicity and distrust it. (A.N. Whitehead)

Learned people who insist on the supremacy of their own theory, no matter what the circumstances, turn it into a dogma that suppresses thinking, in favor of indoctrination. Let's take the example of a theory from economics that once brought us great wealth but is now destroying our societies (a myth I discuss in *Rebalancing Society*): essentially, that greed is good, markets are sufficient, and governments are suspect. As one view of human nature, this makes some sense. As *the* view of human nature, it is nonsense. Where is community? Where is benevolence?

Theory as Practical

Some people who call themselves "practical" poo-poo theory as impractical. But we can no more get along without theory than can we get along without files on the Internet, because theories, likewise, help us to organize incoming information. As John Maynard Keynes quipped, "Practical men, who believe themselves to be quite exempt from any intellectual influences, are usually the slaves of some defunct economist."

It would be nice if we could carry reality around in our heads, and use it to make decisions and manage. Unfortunately, no head is that big. So, we carry around theories instead, consciously or not, alongside our own cumulation of experiences. But, for the sake of thoughtfulness, we must carry around various theories, not any one best theory, to be able to choose the most useful under the circumstances. As F. Scott Fitzgerald put it, "[T]he test of a first-rate intelligence is the ability to hold two opposed ideas in the mind at the same time, and still retain the ability to function." If only managers could keep it to two!

Our Myths and deMyths as Theories

The myths of this book are theories in their own right, or else they build on some theory. For example, business as the one best way is built on the claim that governments are suspect. So, don't get mystified by any claims about truth in this book, and that includes the deMyths as well as the myths. Recognize that all can sometimes be useful and sometimes not. Strategic planning, for example, may be fine when an organization needs to program a strategy that is working well, just as communityship should be suspect when it encourages groupthink. We have to keep our minds open for the next good theory that comes along, bearing in mind that it, too, could eventually turn out to be mythical.

Two Insights to deMYTHtify Truth

We finish this book with two Insights to help us deal with all the reframing called for in the book. One is about developing playful solutions for puzzling problems, and, if this sounds daunting, the other is about how such solutions can emerge from the ordinary creativity that all of us exhibit every day.

Playful Solutions for Puzzling Problems[89]

We are great with pat answers but awful with puzzling questions. Faced with a daunting problem, we zero in on some established solution: keep two meters distant in a pandemic,[90] fix capitalism in a broken democracy.[91] Many puzzling problems require playful exploration.

Let's distinguish the pat from the puzzling. A jigsaw puzzle is about as pat as a game can get: connect the proper pieces while respecting the proper rules to make the proper picture. My dictionary defines *puzzle* as "a difficult or confusing problem." In fact, jigsaw puzzles are hardly that, but puzzling puzzles are. Beyond just breaking the rules, puzzling puzzles get around old rules that no longer work. And this requires that we be playful rather than pat, by asking "Why not?" instead of "Why?"

Enough of Pat Solutions for Puzzling Problems

Why are we so fixated on pat solutions for puzzling problems? Has pat schooling killed our creativity, or might it be because we play so many games that come in boxes—cardboard or electronic—while we rattle on about "thinking outside the box"?

In a Pat Puzzle	In a Puzzling Puzzle
1. The pieces are supplied.	1. The pieces have to be created.
2. Each is clean-cut.	2. They begin as fragments, obscure.
3. They fit together perfectly.	3. They connect loosely, if at all.
4. They make the picture shown on the box.	4. With no box in sight, the picture has to be constructed from these fragments and connections.

We used to play more playful games, like Charades, while the kids were using LEGOs to build their own thing, instead of assembling three-dimensional jigsaw puzzles.

Beyond games, consider how much of management, medicine, politics, and life has succumbed to pat categorization. Diagnose that patient into a designated disease with its designated protocols. Slot that voter into an established market segment. "Downsize" thousands of workers when you miss your numbers.

Some of this may be fine when an existing category fits. Hail to those protocols and segments that work. But problems fester when the fit is forced. A patient falls between the cracks of medical specialties.[92] Voters get minds of their own. As for all that downsizing, the fault, dear leaders, may lie in you stars at the top, who perhaps upsized too quickly. (See MythSite.org/downsizing.) So, let's get playful, and challenge the categories that box us in. And here comes the easy part: all this requires is a bit of ordinary creativity.

Ordinary Creativity Can Be Extraordinary[93]

It is thrilling to listen to Tchaikovsky's Violin Concerto. The creativity is amazing; how many people are capable of that? But there is another kind of creativity of which we are all capable. It's quite ordinary, in fact, although the consequences can be extraordinary. This is the creativity that changes the world.

Let me explain with a joke I once heard. "I'd like to die like my grandfather died—quietly, in his sleep. Not like those other people in the car who died yelling and screaming." We picture grandpa in bed, but he was actually behind the wheel of the car. It's just a little switch really, which is what makes it a joke.

Jokes, of course, don't change the world. (Nor did Tchaikovsky's Violin Concerto, for that matter.) But how about this little switch: In 1928, microbiologist Alexander Fleming was researching antibacterial agents in his London laboratory. Returning there after vacation, he noticed that mold had killed some bacteria in one of his plates. Standard practice was to discard such samples—they are anomalies, after all—and carry on, which Fleming did. But following a conversation with a colleague, he took that sample out of the trash, to consider if this mold could be used to kill destructive bacteria in the human body. This was the critical moment, the key little switch that changed the world. What was trash became one of the great medical discoveries of all time. Just like that IKEA switch, which changed the furniture business.

Maybe you have never created a great violin concerto. But I'll bet you have come up with your share of little jokes. Well then, by switching that playfulness to something more serious, you, too, can change the world.

Additional Insights Available on MythSite.org

Myth 1

Transformation by Lofty Leadership or by Engaged Management?

Myth 2

Working Like a Cow by Walking Like a Cow

Selecting Flawed Managers

Organigraphs: Seeing the Organization for What It Is

From Organizational Boundaries to Outward Bound

Myth 3

The Programming Imperative

Business as the Best Way?

Myth 4

Enough of MORE. We Need Better: How Stock Markets Kill Companies and Communities

Myth 5

Reaching Out to Social Learning

Stories from Developing Naturally

Myth 6

Networks Are Not Communities

Myth 7

Analyst: Analyze Thyself

Productive and Destructive Productivity

Porterian vs Peterian Effectiveness

Myth 8

The Honda Story, as Learning Before Planning

Some Notes About Strategy

Imaging Strategy

Myth 9

Seeing Every Which Way

Zooming Ahead? Not So Fast!

Myth 10

Downsizing as 21st-Century Bloodletting

Notes

1. Stephen Piersanti, "The 10 Awful Truths about Book Publishing," https://ideas.bkconnection.com/10-awful-truths-about-publishing.

Myth 1

2. W.G. Bennis, *The Unconscious Conspiracy: Why Leaders Can't Lead* (AMACOM, 1976), also W.G. Bennis, *Why Leaders Can't Lead: The Unconscious Conspiracy Continues,* (Jossey-Bass Publishers, 1989).
3. M. Augier, *James March on Education, Leadership, and Don Quixote: Introduction and Interview,* (Academy of Management Learning & Education, 2004), 3(2), 169–177.
4. Adapted from "A CEO Letter to the Board . . . Long Overdue," mintzberg.org/blog. July 29, 2017
5. Adapted from "Managing Scrambled Eggs," mintzberg.org/blog. October 17, 2018.

Myth 2

6. J. Smith, K. Walshe & D.J. Hunter, "The 'Redisorganisation' of the NHS: Another Reorganisation Involving Unhappy Managers Can Only Worsen the Service," *British Medical Journal*, 2001, 323 (7324), 1262–1263.

7. Sally Helgesen, *The Female Advantage: Women's Ways of Leadership* (Crown Currency, 1990), 45.

8. Henry Mintzberg, "Leadership and Communityship: Communityship Is the Answer," *Financial Times*, 2006), 23; see also Henry Mintzberg, "Rebuilding Companies as Communities," *Harvard Business Review*, July–August 2009.

9. Edward O. Wilson, *Sociobiology: The New Synthesis* (The Belknap Press of Harvard University Press, 1975), 141.

10. Adapted from "The Epidemic of Managing Without Soul," mintzberg.org/blog. May 21, 2015.

11. Mintzberg, "Killing Communityship..."

Myth 3

12. Henry Mintzberg, *Understanding Organizations... Finally!* (Berrett-Koehler, 2023); discussion of this myth draws broadly from this work.

13. Frederick Winslow Taylor, The *Principles of Scientific Management (*Harper, 1911).

14. Regina E. Herzlinger, "Why Innovation in Health Care Is So Hard," *Harvard Business Review*, May 2006.

15. R.L. Sterba, "The Organization and Management of the Temple Corporations in Ancient Mesopotamia," *Academy of Management Review,* 1 (3), 16–26.

16. Robert W. Keidel, "Football's Out, Basketball's In; A New Game for Managers to Play," *New York Times*, December 8, 1995.

17. Mintzberg, *Understanding Organizations,* 3–5.18. Henry Mintzberg, *The Flying Circus* (Cyan Communications, 2006). Available as a PDF on mintzberg.org homepage. https://mintzberg.org/sites/default/files/book/flying_circus_whole_book_august_2005.pdf.

19. Adapted from "The Best Is Too Low a Standard," mintzberg.org/blog. October 1, 2015.

Myth 4

20. Linda Hill, *Becoming a Manager: Mastery of a New Identity* (Harvard Business School Press, 1992), 15.

21. Draws from Henry Mintzberg, *Simply Managing* (Berrett-Koehler, 2009) and *The Nature of Managerial Work* (Harper & Row, 1973).

Myth 5

22. Henry Mintzberg, *Managers, not MBAs* (Berrett-Koehler Publishers, 2004); discussion of this myth draws broadly from this work.

23. J. Sterling Livingston, "Myth of the Well-Educated Manager," *Harvard Business Review*, January 1971.

24. Andrew Hill, "Harvard and Its Business School Acolytes Are Due a Rethink," *Financial Times*, May 7, 2017.

25. Hill, *Becoming a Manager*, 274–275.

26. Henry Mintzberg, *Rebalancing Society* (Berrett-Koehler Publishers, 2015). Available as a PDF at www.mintzberg.org/books/rebalancing-society.

27. Adapted from Jonathan Gosling & Henry Mintzberg, "The Five Minds of a Manager," *Harvard Business Review*, November 2003.

28. Henry Mintzberg and J. Gosling, "Don't Just Sit There," mintzberg.org/blog. May 2017.

29. Adapted from "Jack's Turn," mintzberg.org/blog. December 5, 2014.

30. Ron Lieber, "Learning and Change—Roger Martin," *Fast Company*, November 30, 1999.

31. F.J. Kelly & H.M. Kelly, *What They Really Teach You at the Harvard Business School* (Warner Books, Inc., 1986), 46.

32. Adapted from "MBAs as CEOs: Some Troubling Evidence," mintzberg.org/blog. February 22, 2017. See the fuller story there.

33. David Ewing, *Inside the Harvard Business School* (Times Books, 1990).

34. Henry Mintzberg and Joseph Lampel, "Do MBAs Make Better CEOs?" *Fortune*, February 19, 2001. See also Mintzberg, *Managers Not MBAs*, 114–118, for some details on these CEOs.

35. D. Miller & X. Xu, "A Fleeting Glory: Self-Serving Behavior Among Celebrated MBA CEOs," *Journal of Management Inquiry*, 25(3), 2016, 286–300. Also, D. Miller & X. Xu, MBA CEOs, "Short-Term Management and Performance," *Journal of Business Ethics*, 154(2), 2019, 285.

Myth 6

36. Henri Fayol, *Administration Industrielle et Générale* (H. Dunod, 1917).

37. Henry Mintzberg, "The Manager's Job: Folklore and Fact," *Harvard Business Review*, 1975.

38. Henry Mintzberg, *Simply Managing* (Berrett-Koehler, 2013), 6.

39. Henry Mintzberg, *The Nature of Managerial Work* (Harper & Row, 1973).

40. M.W. McCall, M.M. Lombardo & A.M. Morrison, *Lessons of Experience: How Successful Executives Develop on the Job* (Simon and Schuster, 1988), 55.

41. Mintzberg, *Managerial Work.*

42. Sune Carlson, *Executive Behaviour: A Study of the Workload and the Working Methods of Managing Directors* (Arno Press, 1955).

43. K.H. Brunsson, *The Notion of General Management* (Copenhagen Business School Press, 2007), 17.

44. Luther Gulick and Lyndall Urwick, eds., "Notes on the Theory of Organization," *Papers on the Science of Administration* (Institute of Public Administration, 1937).

45. L.F. Urwick, "V.A. Graicunas and the Span of Control," *The Academy of Management Journal*, 17(2), 1974, 349–354.

46. Mintzberg, *Managing*, 140.

47. Henry Mintzberg, "Managing as Blended Care," *The Journal of Nursing Administration*, 24(9), 1994, 29–36.

48. Peter F. Drucker, *The Practice of Management* (Harper & Brothers, 1954).

49. Carlson, *Executive Behavior.*

50. L.R. Sayles, *Managerial Behavior* (McGraw-Hill, 1964).

51. Adapted from "The Maestro Myth of Managing," mintzberg.org/blog. January 28, 2019.

52. Mintzberg, *Managing*, 34–41. See also "Managing in the Digital Age: Over the Edge?," mintzberg.org/blog. July 23, 2015.

53. Henry Mintzberg & Peter Todd, "The Offline Executive," *Strategy+Business*, November 27, 2012.

54. Adapted from Mintzberg, *Simply Managing*, chapter 5.

Myth 7

55. Adapted from "The Soft Underbelly of 'Hard Data,'" mintzberg.org/blog. July 9, 2015.

56. Abraham Kaplan, *The Conduct of Inquiry* (Chandler Publishing Company, 1964).

57. Josiah Stamp, *Some Economic Factors in Modern Life* (P.S. King & Son, Limited, 1929).

58. Henry Mintzberg, *Managing the Myths of Health Care* (Berrett-Koehler, 2017), 67, with Sholom Glouberman.

59. Mintzberg, *Rebalancing Society.*

60. Henry Mintzberg, "Reorganising Our Heads for the Care of Our Health," *BMJ Leader*, 8(4), e000912.

61. "How National Happiness Became Gross,'" mintzberg.org /blog. August 29, 2018. All references and quotes in this Insight can be found here.

62. Henry Mintzberg, "A Note on that Dirty Word *Efficiency*," *Interfaces* 12 (5), 101–105.

63. E.G. Malmlow, "Corporate Strategic Planning in Practice," *Long Range Planning*, 5(3), 2–9.

Myth 8

64. Tony Jackson, "The Dirty Little Secret of Strategy," *Business Standard,* May 13, 1997.

65. Henry Mintzberg, *Rise and Fall of Strategic Planning* (Simon and Schuster, 1994).

66. Michael E. Porter, "The State of Strategic Thinking," *Economist*, May 23, 1987, 21.

67. Henry Mintzberg, "The Strategy Concept I: Five Ps for Strategy," *California Management Review*, 1987, 13.

68. Micheal E. Porter, *Competitive Strategy* (Free Press, 1980); Micheal E. Porter, *Competitive Advantage* (Free Press, 1985).

69. Peter F. Drucker "The Theory of the Business," *Harvard Business Review*, 72(5), 1994, 95–104.

70. Henry Mintzberg, *Tracking Strategies* (Oxford University Press, 2007).

71. "Small Ideas, Big Dreams," *The Story of Ikea Flatpacks* web page, effective February 4, 2026, https://www.ikea.com/ph/en/this-is-ikea/about-us/the-story-of-ikea-flatpacks-puba710ccb0/.

72. Henry Mintzberg & Alexandra McHugh, "Strategy Formation in an Adhocracy," *Administrative Science Quarterly*, 1985, 160–197.

73. Henry Mintzberg & James A. Waters, "Tracking Strategy in an Entrepreneurial Firm," *Academy of Management Journal*, 25(3), 1982, 465–499.

74. Adapted from "Need a Strategy? Let Them Grow Like Weeds in the Garden," mintzberg.org/blog. June 29, 2018.

Myth 9

75. Henry Mintzberg, Duru Raisinghani & Andre Theoret, "The Structure of 'Unstructured' Decision Processes," *Administrative Science Quarterly*, 1976, 246–275.

76. Alexander Kotov, *Think Like a Grandmaster* (Batsford, 1971).

77. W. Köhler, *The Mentality of Apes* (Routledge, 1925).

78. Karl E. Weick, *The Social Psychology of Organizing* (Addison-Wesley, 1969).

79. Terry Connolly, "On Taking Action Seriously," In G.N. Undon & D.N. Brunstein (Eds), *Decision-making: An Interdisciplinary Inquiry* (Kent Pub Co., 1982).

80. Peter Drucker, *Management: Tasks, Responsibilities, Practices* (Harper & Row, 1974).

81. Robert E. Ornstein, *The Psychology of Consciousness* (Harcourt Brace Jovanovich, 1977), 59.

82. Henry Mintzberg, "Planning on the Left Side and Managing on the Right," *Harvard Business Review*, July 1976.

83. H. A. Simon, *The Sciences of the Artificial* (M.I.T. Press, 1969).

84. Mintzberg, *Understanding Organizations*. Adapted from chapter 21.

85. Henry Mintzberg & Jeanne Liedtka, "Time for Design," *Design Management Review*, June 2010, 17(2), 10–18.

86. From Gordon Siu, told in J. Peters & R.H. Waterman, *In Search of Excellence* (Harper & Row, 1982).

87. "What Is Design Thinking?" *IDEO* web page, effective February 4, 2026, https://designthinking.ideo.com/.

88. Adapted from Henry Mintzberg, "Is Serendipity Serendipitous?" *Journal of Management Inquiry*, 35(1), 2026, 19–21.

89. Adapted from "Playful Solutions for Puzzling Problems," mintzberg.org/blog. October 18, 2020.

90. See "Can Pollution Be a Missing Piece in the Pandemic Puzzle?" on mintzberg.org home page.

91. Adapted from "Getting Past the Adjectival Capitalism Fix," mintzberg.org/blog. October 17, 2014.

Myth 10

92. Mintzberg, *Managing the Myths of Heath Care*, 52–60.

93. Adapted from "The Extraordinary Power of Ordinary Creativity," mintzberg.org/blog. March 5, 2015.

Index

Acting, the ambiguity of, 80
Action mindset, 55, 64. *See also* Thinking, seeing, and doing
Action plane, 68
Adams, Brian, 66, 72
Airlines, 34–36. *See also* Eastern Airlines
Analysis. *See also* Measurement
  intuition and, 117–118
Analytical mindset, 55, 100
Anomalies, cherishing, 125
Art/craft/science triangle, 42–49, 46t, 47f

Balanced scorecard, 88
Bennis, Warren, 5, 106
Bentz, Jacques, 72
Bernier, Sylvie, 36
Bhutan, 89–90
"Big picture," seeing vs. losing sight of the, 5, 7–8
Broad perspective, strategy as, 102, 103f
Bureaucracy, 2, 24–26, 34–36. *See also* Programmed organizations
  imperatives of, 24
Business. *See also* Private sector business
  vs. management, 49–50
Business education, 51–52. *See also under* MBAs
  vs. management education, 49, 53–54

Calculated chaos, managing as, 66
Calculating style of managing, 43, 66
Carlson, Sune, 63–64, 74–75
Central management, 18f
Cerebral hemispheres, 118–119
Cerebral management, 43–44
Chain of command, 17–18, 17f, 26. *See also* Programmed organizations
Change, the riddle of, 80
Chaos. *See* Calculated chaos
Chief executive officers (CEOs), 61–63
  letter to the board from a CEO, 9
  MBAs as, 58–60
Chimpanzee experiment, Köhler's, 115
Churchill, Winston, 112, 129
Cleghorn, John, 5, 72
Collaboration, 30
Collaborative mindset, 55
Columbus, Christopher, 127–128
Commanding. *See* Controlling
Communication
  vs. control, 68
  oral, 65
Communication plane, 69–70
Communityship, 19
  beyond leadership, 19–20
  killing, 22–26
Conducting, characteristics of, 74–76
Confidence, the clutch of, 80
Connecting, the quandary of, 79
Connecting management, 18f
Connolly, Terry, 117
Consolidation, 30
Control
  managers struggle to control their jobs, 61–62
  span of, 66–67

Controlled disorder, managing as, 66
Controlling, 70
  vs. doing, 68
  insights to deMYTHtify managing as, 74–80
  managers as, 61, 62
Conversational approach to design, 121
COVID-19 pandemic, 125
Craft, management as. *See* Art/craft/science triangle
Creativity, 133
  ordinary creativity can be extraordinary, 133

Data. *See* Hard data
Decision making, 113. *See also* Thinking, seeing, and doing
Decomposition, the labyrinth of, 79
Delegating, the dilemma of, 80
Deliberate strategy, 99, 100, 100f, 103f, 104, 109
Design, approaches to, 121
Design thinking/design doing, 122
Devons, Ely, 84
Disorder. *See* Controlled disorder
Distributed management, 20
Doing. *See also* Thinking, seeing, and doing
  vs. controlling, 68
Drucker, Peter F., 74, 102, 117, 118

Eastern Airlines, 11–12
Efficiency, 30, 91–93
  vs. effectiveness, 93
  meaning, 92
  negative connotations, 91, 92
Egg McMuffin syndrome, 101, 102, 102f
Email and managing, 78
Emergent strategy, 99–100, 109
  example of, 105–106
Engaging management, 44
  vs. lofty leadership, 5–6, 8, 8t
Evidence and experience, 39–40, 42
Evidence-based medicine, 39
Evolving approach to design, 121
Ewing, David, 58
Executive MBA programs, 50
Experience and evidence, 39–40, 42

Favoie, Fabienne, 63, 72
Fayol, Henri, 61, 65–67
Fishbowl conversations, 55
Flat Earth, myth of the, 127–128
Flatpack, 105
Flying Circus, The (Mintzberg), 34–35
"Folklore and Fact" article (Mintzberg), 62, 66
"Forest for the trees." *See* "Big picture"
Formulaic approach to design, 121
Formulating strategy. *See* Strategy formulation
Formulation
  failures of, 111
  and implementation, 111

General Motors (GM), 98, 99
Global village, 77–78
Government. *See* Public sector government
Grassroots model of strategy formation, 110–111
Great divide in our brains and organizations, 118–119
Gross National Happiness (GNH), 89
  how national happiness became gross, 89–91
Gullet, Abbas, 44–45, 70

Hamel, Gary, 95
Hard data. *See also* Numbers
  as arbitrary, biased, and distorted, 85
  inadequacy of, 83
  nature of, 85–86
  vs. soft data, 82, 85, 86
  the soft underbelly of, 82–85
  tends to be late, 83
  unreliability of, 83–84

"Hard" formal vs. soft information, 65
Haslam, Carol, 45, 68–69, 71, 73
Health care, 22
efficiency in, 87
misuse of measurement in, 87
Hebb, Donald, 128
Helgesen, Sally, 18
Henschel, Harry, 64
Hierarchical management and leadership, 13–14, 14f, 15f
Hill, Linda, 40, 51–52
Hotels with and without soul, 21–22
Hothouse model of strategy formulation, 109
Hubs, 17f. *See also* Personal organizations

Impact team, 55
Implementation
failures of, 111
stop blaming, 111
Implicit vs. explicit knowledge, 119–120
Individual, leadership as, 6–7
Individualism, meanings of the term, 6–7
Individuality, 35
Inkster, Norm, 71
Insight and decision making, 115
Insightful management, 43
Intended strategy, 97–99, 100f
Internet, impact of the, 76–79
Interruptions and management, 62–64
Intuition
analysis and, 117–118
defined, 118

Judgment, 88

Kaizen, 105
Keynes, John Maynard, 130
Keynote listeners, 55
Kierkegaard, Søren, 100
Knowing, two ways of, 119–120
Köhler, Wolfgang, 115
Kotov, Alexander, 114–115

Lampel, Joseph, 58
Lateral contacts and lateral management, 65–66
Lavoie, Fabienne, 63, 72, 73
Leadership. *See also specific topics*
and being over-led, 6
vs. management, 5–8
nature of, 6, 8t, 49
problems with the concept of, 6–8
Learning mindset vs. analytic mindset, 100
Learning mode, 104–106
Liedtka, Jeanne, 65, 121
Linking vs. leading, 68
Livingston, Sterling, 50
Lofty leadership
vs. engaging management, 5–6, 8, 8t
insights to deMYTHify, 9–10
quintessential story of, 11

Macro-leaders who micro-manage, 7
Management. *See also specific topics*
insights to deMYTHify professional, 44
is not a profession, 40
nature of, 6, 8t
Management education, 49, 53–56. *See also* Business education
Managerial exchanges, 55
Managerial mindsets, 55
Managerial work, characteristics of, 62
fragmentation and interruption, 63–64
lateral contacts, 65–66
oral communication, 65
orientation to action, 64. *See also* Action mindset
the pressures and the pace, 62–63
span of control, 66–67
Managers. *See also specific topics*
developing managers naturally, 53–56
what they might do and must do, 64
who lead, 8

"Manager's Job: Folklore and Fact, The" (Mintzberg), 62, 66
Managers Not MBAs (Mintzberg), 59
Managing
around, 18, 18f
basic managing as fundamental, not fashionable, 24
inescapable conundrums of, 79–80
model of, 68–69, 69f
over the edge, 78–79
roles of, 67–69
communicating all around, on the information plane, 69–70
controlling inside, on the information plane, 70
dealing outside, on the action plane, 72
doing inside, on the action plane, 72
leading inside, on the people plane, 71
linking outside, on the people plane, 71
well-rounded, 72–73
Managing (Mintzberg), 62
MBAs, 55–56
as CEOs, 58–60
insights to deMYTHify the MBA, 56–58
MBA education distorts the practice of management, 48–53
wrong consequences, 52–53
wrong people in the wrong ways, 49–52
McCloskey, Deirdre, 90
McDonald's, 101, 102, 102f
McGill health care management program, 22
McGill University, 107–108
McLuhan, Marshall, 77
Measurement, 81–82. *See also* Hard data
efficiency and, 92, 93
insights to deMYTHify, 89–93
measuring like mad in the public, private, and plural sectors, 86–88
Media and their messages, the, 77–78
Micro-managing vs. macro-leading, 7
Mintzberg, Lisa (daughter), 21

Narcissistic style of managing, 43
National Film Board of Canada (NFB), 105–106
Nature of Managerial Work, The (Mintzberg), 61–62, 119
Neurobiology, 118–119
Numbers. *See also* Hard data; Measurement
quotes about, 89

Omollo, Stephen, 70, 71
Operating management, 18f
Organization no-speak, 34
Organizations
as communal, 6–7
four fundamental forms/species of, 25–26, 25f
beyond the four, an infinite number of ways to organize, 30–31
each has a fundamental force, 30
team sports as each of the, 28–29
types of, 32–34, 33f
Organizing, ways of, 23–26, 30–31
insights to deMYTHtify the one best way, 31
the best is too low a standard, 36–37
one world of organizations, 32–34, 33f
programming the passengers, 34–36
myth of one best way to organize, 23, 24
Ornstein, Robert E., 118–119

Pathways, paving the, 122
Patwell, Beverly, 45
Paving the pathways, 122
People plane, 68–69, 71
Personal organizations, 25f, 26, 29, 30, 43. *See also* Hubs
Perspective, strategy as, 101–103, 101f, 102f. *See also* Strategic perspective

Plan and pattern, position and perspective (four Ps for strategy), 103, 103f
Planning. *See also* Strategic planning
  manager as systematic planner, 62
  the predicament of, 79
Planning mode, 104
"Planning on the Left Side and Managing on the Right" (Mintzberg), 119
Plural sector associations, 33f. *See also* Health care
Porter, Michael E., 90–91, 96, 102
Position, strategy as, 101, 101f, 102f
Practicality and theory, 129–130
Practice, management as a, 42–44, 43f
  stories of, 44–45
Predicting the unpredictable, quotes about, 112
Private sector business, 33f
  overuse of measurement in, 87–88
Problem solving. *See* Puzzling problems
Proficiency, 30
Programmed organizations (chains), 25f, 26–27, 30–31, 44, 104. *See also* Chain of command
Project organizations, 27–30, 105
Public sector government, 33f
  efficiency in, 87
  misuse of measurement in, 86–87
Pure form (of organization)
  danger of, 30
  misfit is the weakness of the, 30
Puzzle, defined, 131
Puzzling problems
  enough of pat solutions for, 131–132
  playful solutions for, 131

Rebalancing Society (Mintzberg), 129
Red Cross Delegation, 44–45, 70
Red Cross delegations for refugee camps, 44–45, 70, 71
Reflective mindset, 55
Reorganizations, 14
Resource allocation, 70
Rise and Fall of Strategic Planning, The (Mintzberg), 96

Sayles, Leonard, 75
Science, 127–128. *See also* Hard data; *specific topics*
  management as. *See* Art/craft/science triangle
  management is not a, 41
  nature of, 42, 46t
Seeger, Pete, 88
Seeing. *See* Thinking, seeing, and doing
Sensemaking, 117
Serendipity
  everyday, 123–125
  expecting, 123
  managing, 125–126
  as serendipitous, 122–123
Sets, 16–19, 17f, 27
Silos in organizations, 15f
  slabs across the, 15–16
Simon, Herbert, 91, 120
Simply Managing (Mintzberg), 62
Slabs (across the silos in organizations), 15–16
Social (vs. economic) costs and benefits, efficiency and, 93
Social learning, 53
Soft data, 82, 85, 86
Soft information, managers cherish, 65
Soul, 19, 21
  hotels with and without, 21–22
Souls of organizations, 19, 21–22
Spherical Earth, 127–128
Steinberg, Sam, 107
Strategic perspective, 102–106, 102f, 104–107. *See also* Perspective, strategy as
Strategic planning, 94, 108. *See also* Planning
  emergent learning beyond deliberate planning, 99–100
  insights to deMYTHify, 109–111
  many pitfalls, one grand fallacy, 96–97
  meanings and uses of the term, 94

Strategic planning *(continued)*
nature of, 94–97, 104
roles of the strategic planner, 95, 95f
situations in which it works well, 104, 130
strategic programming and, 95, 104
Strategic position, 103–108. *See also* Position, strategy as
Strategies
planned vs. learned, 94
as realized patterns, aside from intended plans, 97–98
as tangible positions and broad perspective, 101–103, 102f. *See also* Strategic perspective
tracking, 104–107
Strategy
definitions, 97–98, 101, 102
forms of, 99–100, 100f
scope of the term, 98
Strategy formation, grassroots model of, 110–111
Strategy formulation, 94–95
failures of, 111
hothouse model of, 109
Strategy modes, 103, 103f. *See also specific modes*
Strategy process as planning, learning, visioning, and venturing, 103
Superficiality, 64

Tacit vs. explicit knowledge, 119–120
Tangible positions, strategy as, 102, 103f
Taylor, Frederick, 23, 96
Team sports and forms of organizations, 28–29
Techniques
for developing strategy, 96. *See also* Strategic planning
nature of, 96
Technocrats, 26, 90
Theories, 127–128
our myths and deMyths as, 130
vs. reality, 127
theory as dogma, 128–129
theory as practical, 129–130
Thinking, seeing, and doing. *See also* Thinking first
doing first, 117
quotes about, 116
seeing first, 115, 117
Thinking first, 113–115
insights to deMYTHify having to think first, 120
design doing, 120–122
"Time for Design" (Mintzberg), 121
Tobgay, Tshering (prime minister of Bhutan), 90–91
"Top," "middle," and "bottom" management, 13–14, 14f, 15f
Tovey, Bramwell, 62
Tracking Strategies (Mintzberg), 104
Truth
insights to deMYTHtify, 131
quotes about, 129

Understanding Organizations... Finally! (Mintzberg), 32
Unrealized strategy, 99, 100f
Urwick, Lyndall, 66–67

Venturing mode, 107–108
Vertical chain. *See* Chain of command
Vertical culture, 16. *See also* Slabs
Visionaries, 7, 42, 106, 121
Visionary approach to design, 121
Visioning mode, 106–107

Webs, 16–19, 17f, 27–28
Wharton School Executive MBA program, 50
Whelan, Alan, 45
Why I Hate Flying (Mintzberg), 34–35
Women managers, 18
Worldly mindset, 55

About the Author

Henry Mintzberg is a writer, researcher, and educator, mostly about managing organizations, developing managers, and rebalancing societies (his current focus). This is his twenty-second book, his eighth with Berrett-Koehler. He sits in the Cleghorn Chair of Management Studies in the Desautels Faculty of Management at McGill University in Montreal. Aside from studying, experiencing, and coping with organizations, he spends his private life escaping from them—in canoes (where he collects beaver sculptures), up mountains, and on skates, snowshoes, and a bicycle. He is currently preparing a pamphlet entitled "Balance Now . . . for the Sake of Survival." (See other details on mintzberg.org.)

Berrett-Koehler
PUBLISHERS

Dear Reader,

Welcome to the Berrett-Koehler Community—a global network of changemakers creating positive impact in their lives, organizations, and communities.

Our Mission: Connecting People and Ideas to Create a World That Works for All

We believe transformation is possible. While outdated paradigms of self-interest, exclusion, and hierarchy continue to hold back our communities and organizations, we know that change can happen. That's why we connect people with actionable ideas from leading experts who are already creating the solutions we need.

The BK Way

We're an independent publisher that practices what we publish. Our books, digital resources, and community offerings provide practical pathways for building more just, equitable, and sustainable organizations and lives. Whether you're transforming your workplace, community, or personal practices, our publications meet you where you are with tools that work.

But we don't just talk about positive change—we live it. Through "The BK Way," we put stewardship and purpose before profit. As a benefit corporation, we're legally committed to benefiting all our stakeholders: authors, readers, employees, communities, and the environment.

As our gift to you, claim your free bestselling ebook at bkconnection .com/welcome. You'll also receive fresh leadership insights delivered to your inbox from bkconnection.com/blogs/the-bk-exchange.

You Make the Difference

We're grateful to our readers, authors, and community members, who bring our mission to life every day. Your stories of transformation inspire us and show others what's possible.

Share how BK publications are making a difference in your world at bkconnection.com/impact.

Your friends at Berrett-Koehler

Join the Berrett-Koehler Community

Are you passionate about supporting independent publishing and reading diverse voices and perspectives? Join the BK Community Membership Program and become a part of a vibrant literary community. To support mission-based publishing while saving up to 30 percent on all books and attending exclusive events, visit ideas.bkconnection.com/bkcommunity-join to learn more and become a member.

FSC www.fsc.org
MIX
Paper | Supporting responsible forestry
FSC® C005010